Read and Succeed

Practices to Support Reading Skills in African American Boys

Terry Husband

ROWMAN & LITTLEFIELD EDUCATION

A division of
ROWMAN & LITTLEFIELD
Lanham • Boulder • New York • Toronto • Plymouth, UK

Published by Rowman & Littlefield Education
A division of Rowman & Littlefield
4501 Forbes Boulevard, Suite 200, Lanham, Maryland 20706
www.rowman.com

10 Thornbury Road, Plymouth PL6 7PP, United Kingdom

British Library Cataloguing in Publication Information Available

Library of Congress Cataloging-in-Publication Data

Husband, Terry.
  Read and succeed : practices to support reading skills in African American boys / Terry Husband.
    pages cm
  Includes bibliographical references and index.
  ISBN 978-1-4758-0128-6 (cloth : alk. paper) — ISBN 978-1-4758-0129-3 (pbk. : alk. paper) — ISBN 978-1-4758-0130-9 (electronic) 1. African American boys—Education. 2. Literacy—United States. 3. Boys—Books and reading—United States. 4. African Americans—Study and teaching. I. Title.
  LC2731.H87 2014
  371.829'96073—dc23   2013031349

~

Contents

Foreword

He was four years old, and unlike his brother and sister, who read at three years old, our third child was reading with less enthusiasm. We were particularly concerned about his engagement in stories because he did not care about words on the page (this has only changed recently). In addition, his reading was hampered by his developmental challenges in making the sounds of certain consonants, diphthongs, and diagraphs. You may be thinking that reading at four years old should be commended, and as an early childhood educator, I agree. But it is not just reading that we strove to support in our children; reading engagement was equally important.

As educators who are also parents of African American children in American schools, we know the challenges and pitfalls that have to be navigated to become "proficient" on reading assessments, as well as to garner access to the hegemonic reality of Eurocentric ideals of intelligence. In spite of that reality, we nurtured in our children a love for reading for the sake of relevance, enlightenment, enjoyment, survival, imagination, and information gathering. Yet, our success in our children's reading was supported and nurtured through what we call "our village of readers." The village included family members who engaged our children in reading, the librarian who recommended (and still does) relevant and interesting books, teachers who provided reading inventories to access our children's changing reading interests, and administrators who supported alternative reading assessments (beyond standardized tests) to assess reading proficiency and engagement.

The village of readers is a powerful force in the development of African American children. In this village, there is one goal—and that is to raise a

reader. There is a semiconscious dedication to the nurturing and development of lifelong readers. I say *semiconscious* because while the support is not
staged, it is purposeful, relevant, and impactful. In addition, the members of
the village are critically aware of the plight that African American students,
specifically boys, must endure as they navigate reading in schools. While we
nurtured our village of readers, many African American students have not
had such an opportunity.

Terry Husband, in this timely book, gives us a blueprint to develop a village of readers. His focus on solutions to the systemic problem of low reading
engagement for African American boys is a breath of fresh air. While he provides a framework for the purpose of the book, he does not dwell on the negative aspects associated with African American reading achievement. Rather,
much of the book describes how to support young readers with relevant and
practical information. Largely focused on teachers, Husband provides strategies to improve reading engagement in the classroom and then tackles the
issue of reading curriculum improvements. He also offers strategies to support
change at an institutional level that will affect the culture of school and, ide-
ally, support a critical awareness of reading culture for the school community.

What is most impressive about this book is the attention given to parents.
Husband uses a chapter to support and build a capacity for parents to nurture
their children and collaborate with the school, library, administrators, and
community. Here he displays the blueprint for creating a village of readers and
supports a capacity for schools, families, and communities to augment reading
practices to support African American boys. As a bonus, Husband explores the
often-neglected subject of writing and its relationship to reading engagement. I
have a fundamental belief that we write as well as we read. Thus, if we are going to influence comprehensive reading, we must investigate effective writing
strategies. This point is not lost in this book, as Husband approaches writing
through a culturally relevant framework and does a masterful job at discussing
the intricate relationship with reading and writing.

Not until I read this book did I believe that a village of readers could be
scaled up to encompass a larger set of players. Husband has written another
book that brims with insight, one that could be written only by someone who
has the experiences of a teacher of African American boys as well as the life
experiences of an African American student in American schools. He shows
us all that it takes a village to raise a reader.

Stephen Hancock, PhD
Assistant Director, The Urban Education Collaborative
Associate Professor of Multicultural Education, University of North Caro-
lina, Charlotte

~

Acknowledgments

First and foremost, I thank my Lord and Savior Jesus Christ. I can do nothing without you! I would like to thank my wife, Virlaria, for being my friend, partner, and greatest supporter. I cannot imagine what my life would be like without her continual support, patience, and encouragement. I am truly blessed to have such a loving and caring person in my life. I thank my daughters, Gabby and Elyse, for being pure sources of joy in my life. I thank my mother, Vivian Husband, for always encouraging and supporting me. No one could pray for a better mother on Earth. I thank my dad, Terry Husband Sr., for your selflessness, wisdom, sacrifice, and diligence. In a day and time when so many sons grow up without fathers, I thank you for being a true father in every sense of the word. I thank my brother Terrell for all of your help and support as a younger brother. I have always admired you for being such a strong, independent person.

I thank Cynthia Dillard, Rebecca Kantor-Martin, and Barbara Seidl for demonstrating a way of being within the academy that values all human beings. The seeds that you planted early in my academic career continue to bear fruit to this very day. I thank Rich Milner, Tyrone Howard, and Stephen Hancock for being mentors and role models for me throughout my career. You each continue to make indelible marks on how I think and act within these academic spaces. I thank Michael P. Jackson for being such a sincere friend and brother throughout the years. Thank you for making that "walk" with me time after time.

I thank all of the African American boys whom I have had the pleasure and honor of working with over the years. I believe that I have learned more from you than you probably have learned from me. Finally, I thank all of the dedicated associates at Rowman & Littlefield for all of the hard work and professionalism that went into bringing this project to fruition.

~

Introduction

Room 301: Ms. Reynolds's Third-Grade Classroom

Ms. Reynolds moves to the center of the room. She raises her hand in the air and signals for the students to stop chatting and to begin focusing on her. One by one, the students in Room 301 mimic Ms. Reynolds's hand motion while bringing their conversations to an abrupt end. "I like how everyone is giving me his or her full and undivided attention," she states. The room is completely quiet as the students wait eagerly for her next instructions. "It is now time for us to move into our centers," she announces. The students smile in excitement and anticipation.

Ms. Reynolds begins assigning students to small groups based on assessment data related to their strengths, weaknesses, and interests in reading. She reviews the behavior expectations for students to adhere to while participating at learning centers. "Does anyone have any questions? When I say 'travel,' I would like everyone to move to their centers quickly and begin completing their tasks. Travel!" The students in the classroom promptly transition to various centers. Four African American boys make their way to the kidney table where Ms. Reynolds is standing.

Ms. Reynolds sits down and begins her small group instructional lesson. "Okay, boys, today we are going to learn about a comprehension strategy called 'think-aloud.'" Ms. Reynolds displays a popular piece of children's literature as she models how to "think aloud" while reading. "Now it is your turn! I would like you to read two pages and practice thinking aloud with your partner when I say 'read.' Does anyone have any questions?"

"Why do we have to read these stupid books?" asks Jamal. Ms. Reynolds responds, "We have to read them, so we can become better readers." Keith interjects,

"These books are stupid. These books are for girls!" Ms. Reynolds is disturbed by the boys' brutal honesty. She asks, "Why do you think these books are for girls, Keith?" Keith responds, "None of the people in the story are boys or do the things that boys like me do." Ms. Reynolds leafs through the pages and realizes that Keith's observation is completely accurate.

In an attempt to redirect the discussion, Ms. Reynolds poses a question to Daniel. "What do you think about the books that we read in small group, Daniel?" Daniel responds, "I hate these books. They are all about fake people and fake things!" Ms. Reynolds is a bit confused by Daniel's comment "What do you mean that these books are all about 'fake people' and 'fake things'? People in real life go skiing all the time." Daniel responds in a defensive manner, "Yeah, but me and my family don't do that kind of stuff." Alex joins the conversation, "Yeah, we need more books about the stuff we do at home and in our neighborhood."

Fascinated by the organic discussion that is unfolding, Ms. Reynolds decides to abandon the think-aloud lesson. "Let me ask you boys another question. Do you like to read often at home?" They boys respond simultaneously, "No." Ms. Reynolds explores further, "What do you like to do at home instead of reading?" "I like to play video games!" exclaims Keith. "I like to watch TV and movies!" states Alex. "Why can't we read books about video games and TV?" asks Jamal.

Realizing that it is time for students to transition to the next center, Ms. Reynolds thanks the boys for their active participation in the discussion and announces to the rest of the class that it is time to move to the next learning center. Ms. Reynolds continues to reflect on her discussion with these boys throughout the remainder of the week. Up until that point, Ms. Reynolds never made the connection between reading engagement and the texts that were available for the African American boys in her classroom to read.

Ms. Brown, the building literacy coach, enters the room and begins chatting with Ms. Reynolds about the boys in this group. "How did they do today?" Ms. Reynolds responds, "They are still doing about the same. I think part of the challenge might be the texts that we have been selecting for them to read." Ms. Brown pauses for several seconds and then responds, "That could be true, but don't forget that boys are boys and they typically don't like to read as often as girls!" Ms. Reynolds agrees, "Yeah, I almost forgot about that!" The women spend the rest of their time discussing the progress of the other students in the classroom.

While this vignette is fictional, many teachers who work with African American boys in preK–5 classrooms have had experiences similar to those of Ms. Brown and Ms. Reynolds at one point or another in their teaching careers. This book responds to these issues by presenting a multistrategic framework for teachers, administrators, parents, and other community members to implement while working with African American boys in three contexts.

Who Is This Book Written For?

This book is written for several audiences: preservice teachers, in-service teachers, librarians, administrators, parents/guardians, and community members. First, this book is written for preservice teachers who plan to work in settings with significant numbers of African American boys. It is written to equip them with the knowledge and skills necessary to prevent and combat reading disengagement and underachievement in African American boys. My hope is that preservice teachers will apply the strategies in this book to prevent reading disengagement and underachievement from occurring among the African American boys with whom they will work on a daily basis. In this sense, this book exists as a framework of proactive strategies for preservice teachers to consider and apply as they make their way toward becoming experienced teachers.

Second, this book is written for in-service teachers and reading tutors who currently work with African American boys who are exhibiting reading engagement and achievement challenges. It is written to provide strategies for addressing reading concerns within this population of students. Note that the strategies presented in this book are not meant to substitute the commonly accepted "effective" literacy practices that many classroom teachers and tutors already employ with African American boys. Instead, the strategies presented in this book are designed to complement or augment what is already working in classrooms and schools with respect to African American boys.

Librarians often make important decisions related to the quality and quantity of texts that are available for students to read in school. At the same time, they often play an important role in the kinds of postcurriculum reading-related activities that students engage in (book clubs, literature groups, independent research projects, etc.). Hence, this book is written to encourage librarians to rethink, revisit, and ultimately restructure many of the texts that are excluded or included in school library collections to better meet the needs, interests, and strengths of African American boys.

Fourth, this book is written for administrators as they consider the types of reading interventions and programs that they readily endorse and embrace to support African American boys. Currently, many well-regarded interventions and programs in U.S. schools continue to produce insignificant reading results with African American boys. Hence, this book is written to encourage administrators to examine and embrace alternative ways of supporting African American boys as they become proficient, lifelong readers.

Fifth, this book is written for parents and guardians of African American boys. It is no mystery that parents play a vital role in supporting reading engagement and achievement outside of school. Hence, this book is written to kindly suggest ways that parents and guardians can better support African American boys in becoming fluent readers and lifelong lovers of books. This book is not written to indict parents for what they may or may not be doing to support reading development in African American boys. Instead, it is written to inform and equip parents and guardians with the knowledge and skills needed to further support and extend what is already happening in the homes of African American boys who are fluent readers.

Finally, this book is written for community members who work with African American boys in nonschool-related contexts. Many African American boys in grades preK–5 spend a significant amount of their days in after- and before-school religious, social, academic, athletic, or arts programs and organizations. Consequently, African American boys come into contact with and develop meaningful and caring relationships with many different individuals other than their parents and guardians. This book is written to assist community members (youth ministers, basketball coaches, YMCA after-school program mentors, etc.) in supporting reading engagement and achievement in African American boys.

How Should This Book Be Read?

This book is not intended to be read continuously from cover to cover. Instead, each chapter is designed to be read and discussed (preferably in groups) independent of the other chapters. This will give readers an opportunity to pause and reflect critically on the ideas and concepts presented. A series of discussion questions end each chapter to facilitate group discussions and multiple perspectives on the information and concepts presented. Essentially, this book should be read with multiple individuals and across multiple contexts to promote multiple perspectives and understandings on this topic.

What Makes This Book Distinct and Significant?

Although several fine publications deal with issues of gender and reading, this book is distinct from these in three important ways. First, it is the first of its kind to focus on African American males in preK–5 contexts. Many of the current books on this topic deal with the educational experiences of African American males at the preadolescent stage of development and beyond. Hence, this book provides important insights related to the reading development processes of African American boys in grades preK–5.

The second major distinction is its focus on applied research. Essentially, this book focuses on moving beyond merely describing the challenges that many African American boys face in classrooms and schools with regard to reading development and toward articulating possible solutions to these problems. Not only does this book speak to what is or is not occurring with regard to reading instruction and reading development in and among African American boys, but it also provides strategies related to how these challenges might be addressed.

The third major distinction is the book's focus on mutual participation and engagement among teachers, librarians, administrators, parents, and community members. Much of the previous scholarship on this topic highlights strategies for people who serve African American boys to implement independently. This book differs on this topic because it emphasizes and encourages the collective efforts of different groups of people who serve African American boys on a daily basis.

What Is Reading Engagement and Achievement?

The notion of "achievement" has recently come under scrutiny and criticism from various scholars within the field of education. This criticism is largely based on the fact that achievement, in many contexts, is defined almost exclusively in terms of standardized test data. Taking much of this critique into consideration as well as the fact that multiple factors contribute to children's becoming confident and competent lifelong lovers of reading, this book centers on the broader notion of reading outcomes. "Reading outcomes," as used throughout this book, consists of two closely related concepts: reading engagement and reading achievement.

In short, "reading engagement" is defined as the degree of effort and energy that students voluntarily exert while reading. In this sense, reading engagement can be thought of in terms of how often African American boys read and what level of participation or involvement they put forth while reading. The basic assumption behind this book is that as African American boys voluntarily read more often and read more deeply, they are likely to develop the reading knowledge, skills, and dispositions necessary for them to become confident and competent lifelong readers.

"Reading achievement" pertains to reading performance and reading progress. The five most basic knowledge and performance skills that African American boys must develop to become proficient readers involve phonemic awareness, phonics, fluency, comprehension, and vocabulary. In keeping with these five domains, reading achievement relates to how well African

American boys perform and progress in each area. To this end, some assessments that are commonly used to document performance and progress in each domain are as follows:

> *Fluency*—rubrics, DIBELS (Dynamic Indicators of Basic Early Literacy Skills), oral fluency measures, Multidimensional Fluency Scale, running record, miscue analysis
>
> *Vocabulary*—Peabody Picture Vocabulary Test, Dolch Word List, Fry Word List, cloze tests, sight word list
>
> *Comprehension*—retell rubric, story map, discussion rubric, developmental reading assessment, Fountas and Pinnell Benchmark Assessment, National Assessment of Educational Progress reading assessment
>
> *Phonemic awareness*—rhyme identification checklist, rhyme production checklist, syllable blending checklist, syllable segmentation checklist, syllable deletion checklist, phoneme identification checklist, phonemic isolation checklist, phonemic segmentation checklist, phoneme deletion checklist, phonemic addition checklist, phoneme substitution, Phonemic Awareness Inventory, Yopp-Singer Phoneme Segmentation
>
> *Phonics*—alphabet assessment, phonics survey, phonics, running record, miscue analysis, Word Analysis Inventory, CORE Phonics Survey

Disclaimer about "All" African American Boys

It is important to note here that this book and the concepts therein are not presented in a way that generalizes the experiences of African American boys. Certainly, African American boys are not homogeneous. Hence, the strategies presented here will influence African American boys in different ways and to different degrees. Thus, the strategies should be considered as a collection of possible avenues to increase reading engagement and reading achievement in African American boys.

Also note that "all" African American boys are not exhibiting reading disengagement and underachievement issues. Indeed, significant numbers of African American boys in grades preK–5 are proficient and fluent readers and have a strong affinity for texts. In no way, form, or fashion is this book written to suggest that all African American boys are facing reading engagement and reading achievement challenges.

What is in each chapter?

Chapter 1 provides a close and in-depth look at the reading performance of African American boys in fourth grade on national achievement assessments. In addition, this chapter outlines and defines multiple reading achievement disparities that exist between African American boys and other student groups (African American girls, white males, Hispanic males, etc.). This chapter further compares reading achievement performance between African American boys who qualify for free and reduced-price lunch and African American boys who do not. Finally, this chapter explores the degree to which reading performance in African American boys in fourth grade has changed over the past decade.

Chapter 2 outlines factors that contribute to the reading engagement and achievement issues that exist in African American boys in grades preK–5. As mentioned, African American boys are not homogeneous. Consequently, the factors that contribute to reading engagement and reading achievement concerns in this group are not homogeneous either. Taking this notion into serious consideration, this chapter outlines and discusses a range of factors that contribute to the achievement concerns noted in chapter 1.

Chapter 3 offers multiple strategies for improving reading engagement in African American boys in preK–5 contexts. Drawing from the research on reading engagement, this chapter discusses multiple ways that teachers can increase reading engagement in their classrooms. Practical strategies for teachers to implement are presented.

Chapter 4 outlines and discusses a multistrategic framework for teachers, schools, and administrators to implement systematically and simultaneously to improve reading achievement in African American boys. This chapter begins by discussing strategies that teachers can implement within the classroom context to improve reading achievement in African American boys. Next, the chapter discusses strategies to implement within the curriculum to improve reading achievement in this group. Third, it presents and discusses strategies to implement at the institutional level.

Reading and writing are reciprocal processes. Essentially, reading affects students' writing development, and writing affects their reading development. Consequently, chapter 5 outlines and discusses strategies for improving writing engagement in African American boys in preK–5 contexts. Strategies are presented for incorporating culturally relevant and popular culture themes within writing instruction. Additionally, strategies are offered for supporting African American boys while writing in twenty-first-century modes and mediums.

Chapter 6 is aimed at supporting parents/guardians and other community members in improving reading outcomes in African American boys, in two ways. This chapter discusses strategies that teachers, librarians, and administrators can implement to equip parents/guardians and community members with the skills, knowledge, and attitudes necessary to work toward improving African American boys' literacy outcomes. In this sense, this chapter focuses on initiatives and programs started and led by teachers, librarians, and other key school officials. Next, it discusses strategies that parents/guardians and other community members can implement in their respective contexts. In this sense, this chapter focuses on initiatives and programs started and implemented by parents/guardians and other key community members.

Appendix A provides a list of selected pieces of children's literature that contain African American males as main characters in the text. This list provides a short summary of the events in each text and the author information. It is provided to support teachers, librarians, administrators, parents/guardians, and other community members in identifying texts to use while applying the strategies presented throughout this book. Appendix B provides an example of a "choice board" that teachers might use to differentiate instructional activities with African American boys. Appendix C provides examples of graphic organizers that African American boys might use while reading, to add to their comprehension. Appendix D provides a sample "reading interest inventory" that teachers might use to assess the interests of African American boys.

CHAPTER ONE

~

Reading Achievement in African American Boys

Over the past decade, multiple initiatives (e.g., No Child Left Behind, Response to Intervention, Race to the Top, Common Core) have been implemented to improve reading achievement outcomes in underperforming students. While many of them acknowledge the existence of an "achievement gap" between students of color and white students, little has been discussed about the extent to which African American males do or do not perform at comparable levels in reading as other student groups.

A close examination of student performance on national reading assessment measures indicates that by the fourth grade, multiple reading achievement gaps exist between African American boys and other student groups. These gaps pertain to race, gender, and social economic status. This chapter examines and discusses in great detail different reading achievement gaps between African American boys and other student groups.

Note that the purpose of this chapter is not to advance a "deficit discourse" on reading achievement in African American boys. Instead, its purpose is to provide a general understanding of the status of reading achievement in African American boys in fourth grade across the United States. The data presented here should not be interpreted as being applicable to every African American boy in fourth grade in every educational context. Instead, the data should be interpreted as a general overview of reading achievement in African American boys in fourth grade in the United States.

While I completely acknowledge the issues and shortcomings inherent in and associated with using standardized test data as the sole indicator of achievement in any group of students, data from the National Assessment of Educational Progress (NAEP) measure in reading will nonetheless be used and referenced throughout this chapter. This is due primarily to its ability to generate data about reading achievement in African American boys across multiple educational contexts in the United States.

African American Boys and Other Groups of Boys

Recent data from the National Center of Education Statistics (2011) reveal that African American boys in fourth grade performed significantly lower than most other racial groups of boys in fourth grade on the NAEP measure in reading. Specifically, African American boys in fourth grade earned an average score of 200 on the NAEP measure in reading. White boys in fourth grade earned an average composite score of 228 on the NAEP measure in reading. On this same assessment, Asian boys earned an average composite score of 233, while Hispanic boys earned an average composite score of 203 and Native Hawaiian/Pacific Islander boys earned an average composite score of 213. Furthermore, African American boys in fourth grade performed slightly higher than American Indian/Alaska Native boys, who earned a composite score of 196 on this assessment measure.

These data underscore two daunting facts about reading achievement in and among African American boys in fourth grade. First, these data point out that by fourth grade many African American boys are already performing

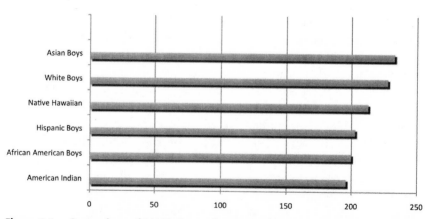

Figure 1.1. Comparison of NAEP Scores between African American Boys and Boys from Other Racial Backgrounds.
Adapted from U.S. Department of Education National Assessment of Educational Progress in Reading, 2011

nearly 28 points lower than white boys on this assessment measure. Next, this data set reveals that many African American boys in fourth grade are performing lower than most of the other racial groups as well. Last, these data point out the existence of an achievement gap between African American boys in fourth grade and boys from other nonwhite groups.

African American Boys and Girls

Generally speaking, girls tend to outperform boys on most reading measures. This trend is quite evident when we compare the reading performance scores of African American boys in fourth grade with the reading performance scores of fourth-grade girls from various racial backgrounds. For instance, in 2011, Asian girls in fourth grade earned an average composite score of 239 on the NAEP measure in reading. White girls earned an average of 234. Hispanic girls earned an average composite score of 209, while American Indian/Alaska Native girls scored 208. African American girls in fourth grade earned a composite score of 210 on this assessment.

What do these data tell us? Several important conclusions can be drawn. First, these data indicate that African American boys in fourth grade performed significantly lower than fourth-grade girls from all the other racial backgrounds. Next, these data indicate that the largest gap in reading performance exists between African American boys and Asian American girls in

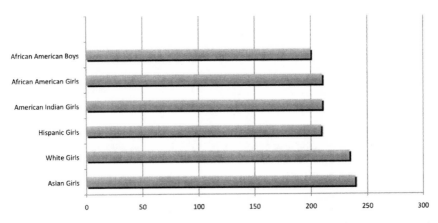

Figure 1.2. Comparison of NAEP Reading Scores between African American Boys and Girls from Various Racial Backgrounds.
Adapted from U.S. Department of Education National Assessment of Educational Progress in Reading, 2011

fourth grade. African American boys in fourth grade scored roughly 39 points lower than Asian American girls in fourth grade.

These data also indicate the existence of a significant gap in reading performance between African American boys in fourth grade and African American girls in fourth grade. In other words, African American boys earned an average composite reading score approximately 10 points lower than the average composite reading score of African American girls.

African American Boys and Social Economic Status

Reading achievement gaps also exist between African American boys in fourth grade who do and do not qualify for free and reduced-price lunch. In 2011, African American boys who qualified earned an average composite score of 195 points on the NAEP measure of reading achievement. At the same time, African American boys who did not qualify earned an average composite score of 216 points on this measure.

When social economic status remains a constant variable, African American boys in fourth grade still do not perform at the same level as fourth-grade boys from most other racial groups. White and Asians boys in fourth grade who were eligible for free or reduced-price lunch earned an average composite score of 213 points on this measure. Hispanic boys in fourth grade who were eligible earned an average composite score of 199, while American Indian boys in fourth grade who were eligible earned a score of 189.

Two important conclusions can be drawn from these data. First, socioeconomic status plays a significant role in reading achievement outcomes

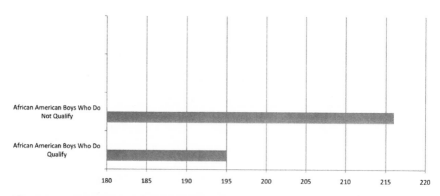

Figure 1.3.   Comparison of NAEP Reading Scores between African American Boys Who Do and Do Not Qualify For Free or Reduced Lunch.
Adapted from U.S. Department of Education National Assessment of Educational Progress in Reading, 2011

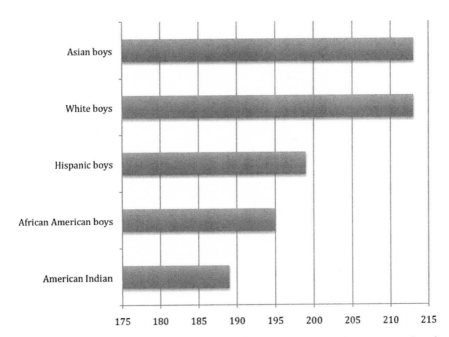

Figure 1.4. Comparison of NAEP Scores of Boys Who Are Eligible for Free or Reduced Lunch.
Adapted from U.S. Department of Education National Assessment of Educational Progress in Reading, 2011

between African American boys in the fourth grade who are and are not eligible for free and reduced-price lunch. African American boys who qualified earned an average composite score of nearly 18 points lower than African American boys in fourth grade who were not eligible. These data also point out the existence of reading achievement disparities between fourth-grade African American boys and fourth-grade boys from other racial backgrounds who share the same socioeconomic status.

African American Boys in Private Schools

In 2011, African American boys in fourth grade in national private schools earned an average composite score of 203 in reading on the NAEP. At the same time, Asian boys earned an average composite score of 236 and American Indian boys earned a score of 198, while white boys earned an average composite score of 237 and Hispanic boys earned a score of 222.

Three important conclusions can be drawn from these data. First, African American boys in fourth grade in national private schools are not performing

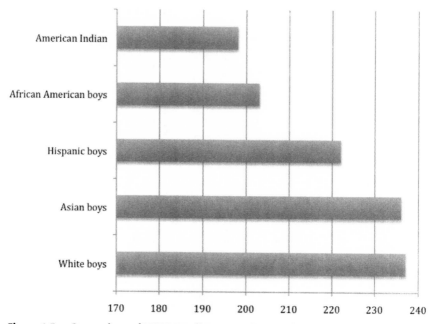

Figure 1.5. Comparison of NAEP Reading Scores between Boys in Private School Settings.
Adapted from U.S. Department of Education National Assessment of Educational Progress in Reading, 2011

at the same levels in reading as most other comparable groups of boys. In this sense, the private-school context does not seem to be making a significant impact on decreasing the reading achievement gap between African American boys in fourth grade and other groups of boys. Next, these data indicate nearly a 33-point reading achievement disparity between African American boys and white boys in fourth grade in private schools.

Reading Achievement Over Time

How have reading achievement outcomes in African American boys in fourth grade changed over the past decade? They have remained largely constant. With the exception of a slight increase in reading achievement between 2005 and 2007, African American boys in fourth grade have demonstrated relatively small achievement gains over the past ten years. For instance, in 2005 African American boys in fourth grade earned an average composite score of 195 on the NAEP measure in reading. Two years later, in 2007, African American boys in fourth grade earned an average composite

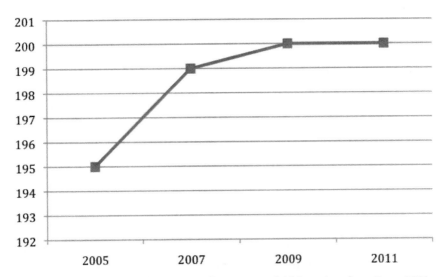

Figure 1.6. Comparison of NAEP Reading Scores of African American Boys, 2005–2011.
Adapted from U.S. Department of Education National Assessment of Educational Progress in Reading, 2005–2011

score of 199. In 2009, they earned an average composite score of 200. Finally, as mentioned, African American boys in fourth grade earned an average of 200 in 2011.

What conclusions can be drawn from these data? Two important ones. First, these data indicate that African American boys in fourth grade have made some positive gains in reading achievement scores over the past ten years. Next, these data indicate that these gains have been very small.

Key Points to Remember

This chapter examines reading achievement in African American boys and other student groups in fourth grade. The following is a brief summary of the data presented:

- There is a significant gap in reading achievement between African American boys in fourth grade and fourth-grade boys from most other racial groups.
- There is a significant gap in reading achievement between African American boys in fourth grade and girls in fourth grade from all the other racial groups.

- Reading achievement disparities exist between African American boys in fourth grade who do and do not qualify for free and reduced-price lunch.
- Racial disparities continue to exist in reading achievement even when socioeconomic status remains a constant variable.
- Reading achievement disparities exist between African American boys in fourth grade and boys in fourth grade from other racial groups in private school contexts.
- Reading achievement in African American boys in fourth grade has increased slightly over the past ten years.

Reflection and Discussion Questions

- What were your initial reflections and reactions to the various reading achievement gaps presented in the chapter?
- Which of the aforementioned reading achievement gaps is most apparent in your respective educational context?
- What do the statistics presented in this chapter imply about reading instruction in grades K–3?
- What do the statistics presented in this chapter imply about reading instruction in grades 5–12?
- To what extent do you think these trends in reading achievement in African American boys in fourth grade will change or remain the same over the next decade? Why?

CHAPTER TWO

~

Factors That Contribute
to Reading Disengagement
and Underachievement

As mentioned, African American boys are not all the same. They bring diverse interests, abilities, strengths, and background experiences into the classroom. At the same time, African American boys in preK–5 classrooms interact with different teachers, curricula, texts, and peers in different schools. As a result of these differences, there are multiple factors that affect reading disengagement and underachievement in this group.

This chapter outlines a myriad of these factors. While not exhaustive, it discusses reasons associated with

- Reading attitudes
- Reading preferences
- Social and cultural inconsistencies
- Pedagogical issues
- Societal norms and expectations
- Neurological differences in the brain
- Curriculum issues
- Institutional practices, policies, and procedures

It is important to reiterate at the outset that African American boys are not monolithic. Thus, each factor discussed affects African American boys in varying degrees. For instance, while some African American boys are more heavily influenced by curriculum- or gender-related issues, others might be more heavily affected by institutional- or teaching-related issues. Hence, readers should read each factor as "possible" causes.

Reading Attitudes

There is a strong connection between a student's attitude toward a particular subject or activity and the amount of effort and energy that he or she will exert while engaged in it. In other words, students who have positive attitudes toward math, science, and social studies are more likely to put forth more effort and energy during these subjects than students who have negative attitudes toward them. In like manner, students who have positive attitudes toward reading and writing are likely to read and write more often and to a greater degree than students who have negative or impartial attitudes toward reading and writing.

Generally speaking, girls tend to have more positive attitudes toward reading than do boys (Merisuo-Storm 2006). Girls often associate reading and reading-related activities (responding, discussing, inferring, etc.) with positive emotions, thoughts, and states of being. In contrast, boys tend to associate reading and reading-related activities with negative or impartial feelings. Due to these differences in reading attitudes, girls tend to read more often than boys.

There is a positive relationship between the amount of time that a child spends reading and how well he or she performs on various reading assessments. Largely, students who read frequently tend to perform higher on reading assessments than students who read infrequently. In this vein, many African American boys are disengaged during reading simply because they have negative or impartial attitudes toward reading. Over time, these attitudes can impede their reading motivation, frequency, and achievement.

Reading Preferences

Boys and girls tend to have different reading preferences (Davila and Patrick 2010). Boys tend to prefer reading books related, but not limited, to the following themes:

- Nonfiction
- Action
- Scary fairy tales
- Superheroes

- Humor
- Science fiction
- Sports
- Hobbies
- Video games

Also, boys tend to prefer reading texts that have a male character as the main character. In contrast, girls tend to prefer reading texts that relate to the following themes:

- Fiction
- Romance
- Mystery
- Narrative experiences
- Pleasant fairy tales

Unfortunately, many early childhood classroom libraries consist of texts that speak more to the interests of girls than boys. As a result, many boys are often unmotivated to read the texts that are available at school. Again, there is a direct relationship between reading frequency and reading proficiency. Essentially, children who read often tend to develop reading skills faster than children who read infrequently. For that reason, African American boys are less likely to read if they do not have texts that are consistent with their reading interests.

Not only do boys and girls often differ in the types of texts they prefer to read, but they also prefer to read for different purposes and in different ways (Logan and Johnston 2010). Generally speaking, boys tend to prefer reading for analytical, practical, informational, and directional purposes. In other words, they tend to examine and comprehend the "nuts and bolts" of the text. Conversely, girls tend to prefer reading in ways and for purposes that allow them to examine, analyze, and discuss the literary or aesthetic aspects of a text. Unfortunately, many teachers (consciously or unconsciously) develop and implement reading practices that center more often on the ways that girls prefer to read than the ways that boys do. Consequently, boys often find themselves less motivated to read in many classrooms. Again, this serves as another possible reason why so many African American boys are disengaged and/or underachieving in classrooms across the United States.

To illustrate, Ms. Rice is a first-grade teacher at Carville Elementary School. During story time, she typically selects classic texts, such as *Little Red Riding Hood*, *Cinderella*, and *Snow White*. Upon close observation, she notices that several of the African American boys are often disengaged, distracted, and disinterested during this time. After many attempts to redirect this behavior, Ms. Rice decides to have individual conferences with the boys to determine the causes of this behavior. To her surprise, she discovers that the boys are disinterested in the characters and content being presented in the stories.

The following is an excerpt from her conversation with a six-year-old African American boy in her class named Jason:

MS. RICE: How are you, Jason?

JASON: Good!

MS. RICE: I just had a few questions to ask you about story time. Is that okay?

JASON: Yeah.

MS. RICE: I noticed that you and a few of your friends were not really focusing on the book during story time. Can you tell me why, please?

JASON: I didn't like the story.

MS. RICE: Can you tell me what you don't like about the story, please?

JASON: I think it is boring! Plus, I don't like reading about girls and women and girl stuff like that.

MS. RICE: What do you mean by "girl stuff"?

JASON: Like . . . girls in the pictures and girls in the story and stuff about the things girls like to do and how they feel in the story.

MS. RICE: What kind of stuff do you like to read about?

JASON: I like to read about cars and dogs. I just got a new puppy last week!

MS. RICE: Do you think you would be interested in reading books about dogs?

JASON: Yeah!

MS. RICE: Starting tomorrow, I will bring more books about cars and dogs. How does that sound?

JASON: Great!

Much like the boy in this illustration, many African American boys find themselves in situations where they do not have the opportunity to read texts that are consistent with their reading interests as boys.

Social and Cultural Inconsistencies

Students are more likely to engage in texts that reflect their social and cultural experiences than texts that do not (Protacio 2012). With that said, many African American boys are often disengaged from reading at school due to a lack of access to texts that reflect their social and cultural experiences as African American males. Teachers frequently make text selections for their classrooms based on a number of important criteria, such as theme, genre, author, and quality.

The degree to which a particular text is socially and culturally consistent with the experiences of the African American boys in a classroom is usually not a top priority when teachers make text selections. Hence, many African American boys often find themselves disinterested and less motivated to read in the classroom than other students. Again, because there is a direct relationship among reading engagement, reading frequency, and reading performance outcomes, this lack of interest and engagement often translates into lower achievement outcomes for African American boys.

Pedagogical Issues

Two types of pedagogical issues can be linked to reading disengagement and underachievement in African American boys. The first of these issues concerns teaching and learning style discontinuities. African American males tend to respond better to instructional methods that center on interaction, movement, stimulation, and energy (Webb-Johnson 2002). In colloquial terms, African American males respond better in classroom contexts where they "move and groove" instead of "sit and get." Unfortunately, many teachers teach in ways that focus more on the latter approach than the former.

When it comes to reading instruction, many teachers develop and implement lessons that focus more on passive rather than active pedagogical methods. As a result of these teaching and learning issues, many African American boys experience difficulty acquiring the knowledge and skills needed to become proficient readers and lifelong lovers of text.

A second pedagogical issue that contributes to reading disengagement and underachievement in African American boys concerns the way in which reading instruction is taught in many of the classrooms and schools that serve African American boys. Due to ever-increasing pressures to improve student performance on standardized testing measures, reading is often taught in ways that center more on the technical aspects instead of the critical aspects.

Reading instruction is often reduced to "drill and skill" or worksheet-driven activities that do little to encourage critical engagement and connections with texts.

To illustrate, Mr. Thomas is a third-grade teacher in an urban school district in the Midwest. His school's overall performance rating is closely linked to how well his students do on the state-mandated achievement measure given each spring. If the students in the classroom do not make significant gains in reading this year, the entire building staff is subject to being reconstituted.

Diagnostic reading assessments reveal that the students in his class have difficulty identifying the "main idea" in nonfiction passages. In an attempt to address this issue, Mr. Thomas decides to practice it with his class each day for thirty minutes. He gives the students a marker to practice highlighting the main idea in each passage in a test-prep workbook.

Mr. Thomas notices that many of the African American boys in his class are disengaged and even frustrated during the time allotted for reading instruction. Through informal conferences with them, he discovers that the boys' frustrations stem from not being able to interact with books in meaningful and critical ways. Essentially, the strategy that was implemented with the intent of improving these boys' reading achievement actually worked to decrease their levels of engagement with texts in the classroom.

Societal Norms and Expectations

By and large, women in United States tend to read more often than men (Stauffer 2007). As a result, many boys grow up in households, communities, and schools seeing very few males who actively and affectionately engage with texts. Due to a lack of male role models who are readers, many African American boys develop the belief that reading is an activity designated exclusively for girls and women. Thus, many African American boys are often disengaged and unmotivated during reading activities because of a lack of personal and social identification.

Parental expectations can also have an important impact on reading engagement and achievement in African American boys. Children of parents with high academic expectations tend to perform at higher levels in school than children of parents with average or low academic expectations (Baroody and Dobbs-Oates 2011). It is not uncommon for many parents to hold lower academic expectations for male children than for female children. Ultimately, these expectations often affect reading engagement levels in African American boys.

A third way that societal norms and expectations can have a negative impact on reading engagement and achievement in African American boys concerns the conscious and unconscious expectations of teachers. Unfortunately, many teachers have lower reading expectations for boys than girls. These expectations are often translated into low-quality instructional activities for boys (Rashid 2009).

To illustrate, Ms. Washington is a first-grade teacher in a small suburban school district. This is her first year of teaching. Like most first-year teachers, she is both excited and nervous about the beginning of the school year. In an effort to waste no instructional time, Ms. Washington quickly begins teaching the lessons in the basal reading program during the second week of school. All her students work quietly and diligently to complete all the skills-based worksheets that accompany each lesson in the basal reading program.

Ms. Washington begins developing confidence in her ability to teach her students effectively. During parent–teacher conference night, a discontent parent of an African American boy named Jayson Watterson confronts Ms. Washington in her classroom. The discussion ensued as follows:

MS. WASHINGTON: Hello, Ms. Watterson! I'm so glad you could make it here to discuss Jayson's progress tonight.

MS. WATTERSON: Thank you!

MS. WASHINGTON: I am happy to report that Jayson is moving right along in reading. He is completing all of his work and getting most of the answers correct on the reading worksheets. If he continues at this pace, he will probably be reading before the end of the school year.

MS. WATTERSON: Excuse me?

MS. WASHINGTON: In terms of his reading progress, he is right where he should be at this time of the school year. Do you have any more questions for me?

MS. WATTERSON: Yes! I want to know why you assign all of those "baby" books for him to read? We have been in school six weeks, and he keeps bringing home books that he read when he was three years old. He says that a lot of the girls get to read chapter books and he is only allowed to read the books that come with the reading program. He is frustrated and becoming less interested in reading because of this. Did you know that he is reading on a fifth-grade level right now?

MS. WASHINGTON: [*With a look of surprise and embarrassment*] No, I didn't know that. I just thought he needed some of the basic skills. I didn't expect him to be reading above grade level so early in the school year.

MS. WATTERSON: Jayson said that you only allow a special group of girls to read chapter books and to discuss them with each other. Why didn't you take the time to see if he had the ability to read these books as well? I'm confident he is able to read those same books. Plus, he enjoys reading books in that series.

MS. WASHINGTON: I completely apologize to you. I will have the reading coach perform a special reading assessment to determine his reading level and then make the necessary adjustments.

MS. WATTERSON: Thanks. I really appreciate it!

In this illustration, Ms. Washington held lower expectations for Jayson than for the other girls in her classroom. Because of these, Ms. Washington assigned higher-level texts to several girls in the classroom while assigning lower-level texts for Jayson to read. Ultimately, Ms. Washington's expectations had a negative impact on Jayson's progress in reading.

Neurological Differences in the Brain

Recent brain research provides *some* evidence that boys and girls have distinctly different neurological functions and processes (King and Gurian 2006). These neurological differences can have an impact on reading achievement in African American boys. For instance, girls tend to have more neurons in the area of the brain devoted to language development. As a result, girls to develop the oral language skills involved in reading processes more quickly than boys. In many cases, girls are better "wired" than boys to participate fully in English and language arts activities that place a high demand on students' language skills.

Boys and girls also tend to have hormonal differences in their brains that can have an impact on reading achievement. Generally speaking, boys tend to have more testosterone in their brains. At the same time, girls tend to have more estrogen, oxytocin, and dopamine. The hormone testosterone is often responsible for the competitive, active, and somewhat impulsive behavior patterns often seen when boys play and interact with other students in the classroom. Conversely, estrogen, oxytocin, and dopamine tend to produce feelings of satisfaction and contentment in girls.

Having large quantities of testosterone in their brains can make it more difficult for African American boys to sit passively and read independently for long periods. At the same time, having large quantities of estrogen, oxytocin, and dopamine in the brain can make it easier for girls perform the informal skills needed to participate fully in traditional approaches to reading instruction (e.g., read silently for fifteen minutes, practice worksheets, sit and listen to the story, etc.).

Curriculum Issues

The reading curriculum that is implemented in many classrooms in the United States can be attributed to reading engagement and achievement challenges in two important ways. First, the curriculum used in many elementary classrooms tends to have little (if any) focus on the social and cultural experiences of African American boys. In many cases, developmental appropriateness is given much more attention in curriculum design processes than social and cultural appropriateness and relevance.

A second way that the curriculum can have a negative impact on reading engagement and achievement in African American boys deals with the national push toward a standardized curriculum. As mentioned earlier, more and more school districts and early childhood agencies are being required by state and national officials to adopt a standards-based curriculum as a means of increasing student performance on standardized achievement measures.

Unfortunately, many of these standardized curriculum models directly and indirectly encourage teachers to teach all students the same content at the same time. Many of these curriculum models provide early childhood and elementary teachers with few opportunities, tools, and resources to meet the individual and varied needs of the African American boys in their respective contexts. Consequently, many African American boys find themselves participating in reading and writing activities not closely aligned to their individual needs, interests, and abilities.

To illustrate, Mr. Canton is a third-grade teacher in an affluent school district. He recently had an African American boy named Terrell in his class, who transferred into his classroom from the nearby urban school district. Due to a lack of adequate resources, Terrell is reading nearly one grade level behind where he should be at this point in his academic career. Because of ongoing pressure to teach the Common Core standards curriculum in English language arts, Mr. Canton focuses his instruction more on what is identified in the standards document and less on the individual needs of the students in his classroom.

Per the Common Core standards curriculum guide, he is implementing a unit that focuses on comparing and contrasting themes, plots, and settings in literature written by the same author. Through a series of diagnostic assessments, Mr. Canton realizes that Terrell is having difficulty identifying the basic elements in a fiction text. Unless Terrell receives immediate instruction in this area, it will be nearly impossible for him to compare and contrast the themes in multiple texts.

Mr. Canton quickly finds himself conflicted between teaching what Terrell needs and teaching what the school has mandated for him to teach. While discussing this issue with the building administrator, Mr. Canton is strongly encouraged to "teach what will be tested." As such, Mr. Canton proceeds with the unit while making little or no effort to differentiate the lessons to meet Terrell's needs.

Mr. Canton continues in this same vein throughout the school year each time that he encounters other reading skills that Terrell has not yet mastered. As a result, Terrell falls further and further behind. At the end of the school year, Mr. Canton realizes from various reading assessments that Terrell now lacks many of the reading skills, strategies, and processes that are needed for him to read successfully in the fourth grade. What is even worse is that Terrell will enter the fourth grade lacking what he should have acquired in the second and third grades.

Institutional Issues

African American boys are disproportionately affected by many of the discipline and behavior management programs and policies implemented at school. In many schools, African American boys are suspended, expelled, and removed from the classroom for disciplinary-related reasons more frequently than any other group of students (Noguera 2012). Many of these strict "zero tolerance" schoolwide behavior management programs lead to African American boys losing significant amounts of instructional time.

For example, Leon is a second-grade student at Millers Elementary School, St. Louis, Missouri. Due to the "zero tolerance" behavior policy at his school, he was removed from the classroom and sent to the principal's office seven times this year. During these visits, Leon missed a significant amount of classroom instruction related to various reading skills and processes.

Leon's teacher made little or no effort to help Leon acquire the reading skills and processes that he did not learn while spending time out of the classroom in the principal's office. His teacher, Ms. Gooden, more or less believes that it is Leon's responsibility to learn the skills that he missed on his own. By the end of the school year, Leon is reading far behind the other students in his classroom.

A second instructional practice that can have a negative impact on reading engagement and achievement in African American boys concerns what is commonly referred to as "tracking" or "ability grouping" (Lleras and Rangel 2009). Many schools today still place students into static reading groups based solely on their reading abilities. As a result of these practices, many African American boys are often trapped in groups where the focus is on lower-level skills instruction and texts.

Key Points to Remember

This chapter examines various factors that lead to reading disengagement and reading underachievement in African American boys. While not exhaustive, the factors include

Reading attitudes—boys and girls often have different attitudes toward reading that affect how often African American boys engage with texts.

Reading preferences—boys and girls often prefer to read different types of texts and for different reasons. Unfortunately, many preK–5 teachers fill their classroom libraries with texts that speak more to the preferences of girls than boys.

Social and cultural inconsistencies—many preK–5 teachers use children's texts that do not reflect the social and cultural lived experiences of African American boys. Consequently, many African American boys are less engaged with these texts than other groups of students.

Pedagogical issues—many preK–5 teachers teach reading in ways that are inconsistent with the ways in which many African American boys prefer to learn.

Societal norms and expectations—parents and teachers often have and communicate low expectations for African American boys regarding their reading development and progress.

Neurological differences in the brain—boys and girls have different chemicals in their brains that can have some bearing on how they interact with texts and participate during reading instruction.

Curriculum issues—many preK–5 teachers implement a standardized curriculum that makes little or no effort to differentiate to meet the individual needs of African American boys.

Institutional practices, policies, and procedures—many of the building-wide discipline, suspension, and expulsion policies implemented in schools remove African American boys from reading instruction.

Reflection and Discussion Questions

- Which factors discussed in this chapter do you think are most significant? Why?
- Which factors discussed in this chapter do you think are least significant? Why?
- Select one of the factors discussed in this chapter and describe a strategy that you might implement to combat this factor?
- What are some additional factors that might contribute to reading underachievement and disengagement in African American boys?

CHAPTER THREE

~

Principles and Practices for Increasing Reading Engagement

Room 413: Ms. Turner's Second-Grade Classroom

Ms. Turner is a second-grade teacher in a racially and economically diverse school in the Southwest. Many of the teachers in her school think of her as a "highly effective" educator. Yet, Ms. Turner frequently finds herself struggling to keep the African American boys in her classroom engaged throughout her reading lessons.

In an effort to address this issue, Ms. Turner reaches out to the building literacy coach for help. The literacy coach, Ms. Gant, observes Ms. Turner while she teaches a thirty-minute lesson related to "word families." The two women decide to conference about the lesson during an upcoming planning period. The conversation ensues as follows:

Ms. Turner: Thank you for taking the time to visit my classroom and observe my teaching.

Ms. Gant: No problem!

Ms. Turner: What do you think? Did you see what I was referring to when I said that those boys are always off task during reading time?

Ms. Gant: I did notice that they were off task during most of the lesson.

Ms. Turner: So, do you think we need to do some follow-up testing to see if they might have some attention issues?

Ms. Gant: To tell you the truth, I do not!

Ms. Turner: What do you mean?

Ms. Gant: *You might not like what I am about to say next, but I really think the boys are not the problem.*

Ms. Turner: *What?*

Ms. Gant: *I'm not sure if you are aware of this, but you spent roughly twenty-five minutes of the lesson simply talking at the students. You provided very few opportunities for interaction. To be quite frank, the pace of the lesson seemed long and drawn out. Then, to make matters worse, you gave them a worksheet at the end for them to complete independently.*

Ms. Turner: *Wow! I didn't expect all of that.*

As illustrated in this hypothetical scenario, reading engagement plays an important role in how often students read books and the level of effort and energy they voluntarily exert while reading. Multiple factors influence students' motivation and desire to read and engage in texts. This chapter outlines ten key principles that influence reading motivation and engagement in students.

In addition, it offers practical strategies that teachers, administrators, librarians, and other school officials can implement to increase reading engagement in African American boys. Again, African American boys are not all the same. As such, the principles and strategies presented in this chapter will have a varying impact on reading engagement in African American boys. Thus, the strategies should be viewed as possible solutions instead of "silver bullets" that will work for every African American boy every time they are implemented.

Principle 1: African American Boys Should See Value and Meaning in the Texts

Students are more motivated to read when they are involved in reading activities that have personal value and meaningfulness (Gambrell 2011). In other words, students are more enthused and engaged in reading and reading-related activities when they connect to their personal experiences inside and outside school. With that said, African American boys are likely to become more engaged in reading activities if the reading activities presented in the classroom are connected to their lives as both African Americans and boys.

Practical Strategy 1: Implement Reading Activities That Are Racially and Culturally Relevant

One way that teachers can increase reading engagement in African American boys in preK–5 contexts is to develop and implement reading activities that are relevant to the experiences and communication styles of African

Americans in general. Teachers should look for ways of adapting and innovating reading activities to reflect the lived experiences of African Americans in society. African American boys will be more motivated to read when the instructional activities are structured in ways that allow them to make connections between school and out-of-school experiences (Husband 2012).

For example, it is common for many elementary teachers to develop and implement reader's theater scripts as a means of increasing student fluency. Unfortunately, in many classrooms, these scripts do not reflect the personal experiences of African American students. In an effort to increase reading engagement in and among the African American boys in the classroom, teachers might create and implement original reader's theater scripts that reflect the personal knowledge, experiences, and communication styles of the African American students in the classroom.

To ensure a high degree of authenticity, the teacher should solicit information from all the African American students in the classroom. The teacher should also provide opportunities for several of the African American students to assist in constructing the script. Furthermore, by making reading activities such as this one and others relevant to the experiences of African Americans in general, African American boys are likely to be more motivated to read.

Practical Strategy 2: Implement Reading Activities and Texts That Are Relevant to Boys' Interests and Experiences

Another way that teachers can increase reading engagement in African American boys in preK–5 contexts is by implementing reading activities and texts that are relevant to the interests and experiences of boys. As mentioned earlier, boys and girls like to read different kinds of texts. Consequently, boys often become disengaged when they are not provided with ample opportunities to read the types of texts they desire to read (Brozo 2010). Teachers can combat this issue in African American boys by developing and implementing reading activities/texts that are relevant to their interests and experiences as boys (appendix A).

For example, as mentioned previously, boys tend to prefer to read nonfiction books for informational purposes more often than fiction books for entertainment purposes. Nonetheless, there are and will be times when teachers will have to introduce and use fiction texts throughout the reading curriculum to teach specific skills and content. In an effort to increase reading engagement in African American boys during these times, a teacher might provide additional opportunities for African American boys to read nonfiction texts that speak to their interests as boys.

Instead of reading *Cinderella* as an isolated text in the reading curriculum, a teacher might (based on the interests and experiences of the African American boys in his or her classroom) provide additional opportunities for the African American boys to read about castles, kings, or some other nonfiction theme associated with the text. In doing so, the teacher is more likely to keep the African American boys in his or her classroom engaged in the *Cinderella* text.

Practical Strategy 3: Implement Reading Activities and Texts That Highlight the Experiences of African American Males

Another way that teachers can increase reading engagement in African American boys is to implement reading activities and texts that highlight the experiences of African American males in their community and within the larger society. Unfortunately, many African American boys sit in preK–5 classrooms where most of the texts being used do not highlight the experiences of African American males (Giles 2008). In an effort to increase reading engagement and motivation, teachers should strive to incorporate reading activities and texts that highlight the experiences of African American males.

To illustrate, let us suppose Ms. Turner is teaching her students how to identify the main idea in nonfiction texts. She decides to follow the scripted lesson plans from the commercial basal reading curriculum. She notices after lesson 2 that many of the African American boys in her classroom were quite disengaged during the first two lessons. In an effort to increase reading engagement among these boys, she decides to abandon lesson 3 and implement a completely new lesson. The boys share with Ms. Turner that they have a wide range of sports and media interests.

Armed with this information, Ms. Turner goes home and creates a short biographical passage related to the life of Lebron James. The next day during reading class, she explains that the entire class will be learning how to identify the main idea and details in a passage again. As she displays the biographical passage on the SMART board, she notices that the African American boys in her classroom and the other students are now much more deeply engaged in the subject matter being taught.

Principle 2: African American Boys Should Be Permitted to Read a Variety of Texts

Children tend to be more motivated to read when they are presented with a wide variety of texts (Fisher and Frey 2012). In view of this, teachers can increase reading engagement in African American boys by providing a range of reading materials for them to read within the classroom. Because African American boys are not homogeneous, teachers should make sure that the texts are as varied as possible.

Practical Strategy 1: Vary Texts by Genre
It is common for many teachers to use fiction texts in the classroom more often than other genres (Brozo 2010). As a result of this practice, African American boys who are more interested in reading texts that represent other genres are frequently forced to spend a significant amount of time reading texts they are not particularly interested in reading. In an effort to combat this issue, teachers should provide opportunities for African American boys to read across multiple genres.

To illustrate, let us suppose that Ms. Turner is teaching comprehension strategies to a group of African American boys in her classroom. She soon discovers that the boys are somewhat disengaged during the guided reading lesson. When she asks the boys to explain why they did not exert much effort during the lesson, they reveal that they do not like reading "these types" of books. Upon further investigation, Ms. Turner realizes that the boys are referring to fiction books with romantic themes.

After conducting an inventory of the books that are available in her classroom library, she realizes that most of the leveled books that are available for these boys to read at their instructional level are all fiction texts. She decides to remedy this problem by going beyond the classroom library and amassing a collection of fifteen other texts (across different genres) for these boys to read during their guided reading lesson. During the next day, she notices that the boys are now much more engaged during the guided reading lesson.

Practical Strategy 2: Vary Texts by Type
Another way that preK–5 teachers can increase reading engagement in African American boys is by providing opportunities for them to read a variety of types of texts in the classroom. Teachers should provide opportunities for African American boys to read books, magazines, real-life documents, web-based content, and resource materials. Additional examples that teachers might make available in the classroom are:

Wordless books—texts composed exclusively of illustrations and images; very few or no words are involved.

Predictable texts—texts that use a repeated pattern of some type; these may be authentic literature or originally created.

Vocabulary texts—texts that teach and reinforce specific vocabulary concepts and high-frequency words.

Decodable texts—texts that help students learn and practice decoding skills.

Authentic literature—high-quality children's literature selections used to teach a variety of elements and concepts in stories.

Original texts—texts and stories are created by the teacher or students in the classroom.

Practical Strategy 3: Vary Texts by Purpose

Teachers can also increase reading engagement in African American boys by providing opportunities for them to read for different purposes. African American boys are more likely to engage in texts in classrooms where they are encouraged to read for reasons beyond those of mastering basic reading skills and processes. African American boys are also likely to be more engaged and less frustrated in classrooms where every reading activity is not "graded" or assessed by the teacher. Some different purposes for reading include:

Reading for pleasure—when students to are encouraged to read for personal satisfaction.

Reading to get a general impression—when students briefly scan a text to get an overview of the content.

Reading to find facts and data—when students read only parts of a text to find specific facts and data.

Reading to learn—when students read a text in its entirety to comprehend the concepts, vocabulary, and details.

Reading to critique—when students read a text closely while attending to issues of power and injustice.

Reading to review—when students read a text to provide a summary and general evaluation of the text's quality.

Reading to perform a task—when students read to fulfill a series of instructions or directions.

Principle 3: African American Boys
Should Have Multiple Opportunities to Read

Students tend to be more motivated to read when they have multiple opportunities to interact with texts (Miller 2012). With that said, preK–5 teachers can increase reading engagement in African American boys by providing multiple opportunities for them to engage with texts. Teachers should strive to create a classroom environment where African American boys have opportunities to practice their reading skills in a variety of formal and informal contexts.

Practical Strategy 1: Read More Often but for Shorter Periods
Instead of focusing on teaching a single reading lesson that may last twenty to thirty minutes each day, teachers should focus on teaching two or three minilessons that range anywhere from seven to ten minutes. In effect, this will increase the amount of opportunities that African American boys have to interact with different texts. This will also provide more opportunities for African American boys to practice their reading skills and increase their self-efficacy and self-concept as readers. Ultimately, as their self-confidence increases, they will engage in texts more often and to a greater degree in the classroom.

Practical Strategy 2: Integrate Reading across Curriculum
Another practical way that teachers can provide more opportunities for African American boys to interact with texts is to integrate more children's literature across various content areas. Teachers should look for ways to integrate high-quality children's literature in science, social studies, mathematics, and even physical education. Instead of just reading from the official textbook, teachers should provide an ample supply of additonal texts for African American boys to read while learning in these different content areas.

To illustrate, let us suppose that Mr. Smith is teaching his second graders about ecological systems in science. He finds that some of the African American boys in his classroom are disengaged while the class reads about life cycles in the science textbook. In an effort to increase reading engagement, Mr. Smith decides to open each lesson by reading a different children's book related to the scientific concept being explored that day. He begins the unit by reading *A River Ran Wild*, by Lynne Cherry.

To further increase reading engagement, Mr. Smith provides "text sets" related to the concepts being explored for the students in his classroom to read in small groups (based on common interests) and discuss. As a result of integrating additional children's literature within the science curriculum, the African American boys are now much more engaged in reading and learning about ecological systems.

Practical Strategy 3: Provide Extensive Opportunities for Rereading
By and large, children enjoy reading familiar texts. In light of this, rereading familiar and enjoyable texts can increase reading engagement in African American boys in several ways. First, it provides an opportunity for African American boys to practice new skills and processes. Next, it provides an opportunity for African American boys to better understand subtle elements within a story. Finally, it allows them an opportunity to experience the positive emotions that are associated with reading a "good book" again and again. Some methods of rereading familiar texts are as follows:

> *Reread in different ways*—teachers should encourage African American boys to reread familiar texts using different approaches, such as choral reading, echo reading, partner reading, and reading in a funny voice.
> *Reread different times per day*—teachers should encourage African American boys to reread familiar texts all throughout the school day, not just during the times set aside for formal reading instruction.
> *Reread to find new information*—teachers should provide opportunities for African American boys to reread familiar texts to find out new information. Teachers might encourage African American boys to reread a familiar text while posing new questions.

Principle 4: African American Boys Should Have Choice in What They Read

Choice plays an important role in how often students read in most classrooms (Gambrell 2011). Essentially, students tend to be more engaged in classrooms where they are provided with opportunities to select firsthand what they will read than in classrooms where the teacher makes the majority of the decisions. In an effort to increase reading engagement in African American boys, teachers should provide an extensive degree of choice in the classroom.

To illustrate, Ms. Carlton is second-grade teacher who is required by the Common Core standards to teach her students about adjectives. In an effort to increase engagement among the African American boys in her classroom, she provides students with an opportunity to choose the book they would like to read in small group. She informs students that they will vote for their favorite book using sticky notes. Next, she tallies the votes and announces the book that will be used during the small group reading lesson. Instantly, Ms. Carlton notices that these boys are eager to read the book they had input in selecting.

To further increase engagement in a group of African American boys, Ms. Carlton provides a menu of activities for the boys to engage in to practice identifying and using adjectives. The only rule that Ms. Carlton enforces is that the boys must find at least one partner to work with during the activity. Ms. Carlton notices that the boys are now so deeply engaged in the activity that they continue working even after she announces that it is time to clean up.

Practical Strategy 1: Provide Structured Choices
Inevitably, teachers will be required to teach specific reading skills and content directly from time to time. During these instances, teachers should provide opportunities for African American boys to select texts that are related to their personal interests and the Common Core standards. By doing so, teachers are able to attend to the interests, needs, and strengths of the African American boys in their classrooms while attending to the requirements of the standards.

Practical Strategy 2: Provide Interest-Based Choices
Teachers should provide ample opportunities in the classroom for African American boys to read whatever they desire to read. Teachers should even encourage African American boys to bring in texts from home to read in the classroom. Again, African American boys are likely to be more motivated to read when they have access to books that interest them. Teachers should consider administering a reading interest inventory to better assess the interests of African American boys (appendix B).

Practical Strategy 3: Make Recommendations, Not Requirements
Inevitably, teachers will encounter African American boys who are reluctant to make text choices for themselves. In these instances, teachers should provide a list of friendly recommendations for them to follow. Teachers should keep in mind these additional points about choice as they apply the strategies mentioned here.

Too Much Choice Is Overwhelming
If African American boys are presented with too many texts to choose from, they may have difficulty selecting a single text to read for a specific

purpose. Therefore, teachers should provide a reasonable amount of texts to choose from during each activity or lesson.

Provide a Balance between Traditional and Popular Texts
Teachers should keep in mind that African American boys often enjoy reading different texts at home than the texts that are available for reading at school. Consequently, teachers should provide opportunities to read both traditional and popular texts in the classroom.

Scaffold How to Make Appropriate Choices for Specific Purposes
Teachers should take some time and effort to teach African American boys how to make appropriate text choices for themselves. In other words, teachers should teach African American boys how to select texts that are best suited for practicing skills, acquiring information, and personal entertainment.

Provide Some Choice in Activities
Teachers should provide African American boys with an opportunity to choose the activities they wish to engage in to practice the specific reading skills and content being taught. One relatively easy way for teachers to provide African American boys with different activities to choose from during a reading lesson is to create a "choice board" (appendix C).

Provide Some Choice in Assessments
Teachers should provide African American boys with some degree of choice over the ways in which they wish to represent and demonstrate their learning during reading lessons. A relatively simple way for teachers to facilitate this process is by providing a menu of assessment choices for African American boys to use at the completion of a lesson or series of lessons. Teachers should vary the level of assessment difficulty to ensure that the African American boys are being challenged appropriately.

Principle 5: African American Boys Should Be Able to Read in Ways That Are Socially Interactive

Generally speaking, students tend to read more often when reading is presented in a way that involves social interactions among other students (Senn 2012). In light of this, teachers can increase reading engagement and achievement in African American boys by structuring reading lessons in ways that encourage social interaction. Teachers should strive to implement reading lessons and activities that encourage and support social interaction between African American boys and other students within three contexts: classroom, school, and community.

Practical Strategy 1: Make Reading Socially Interactive within the Classroom

One way that teachers can make reading socially interactive in the classroom is by encouraging African American boys to read books in pairs, triads, or small groups. African American boys are more likely to engage in reading if they see reading as more of a "team" activity (like basketball, football, or baseball) than if they see reading as an individual and isolated activity. Some basic ways of making reading socially interactive within the classroom include but are not limited to:

Book *buddies*—when a teacher encourages an African American boy to partner with another person to read books for a variety of purposes.

Book *talks*—short discussions about books that are designed to encourage others to read a specific book in its entirety.

Book *showcases*—when a teacher encourages an African American boy to share a text that he enjoys with the class as a whole.

Book *clubs*—when a group of African American boys meet to discuss and express their feelings and thinking related to shared reading material.

Practical Strategy 2: Make Reading Socially Interactive across the School

In addition to making reading socially interactive within the classroom, teachers should make reading socially interactive within the larger school context. Teachers should work with other teachers and school officials to provide opportunities for African American boys to read texts with other students in other classrooms within the school. Some examples of schoolwide socially interactive reading efforts include but are not limited to:

Before- and after-school literacy programs—when teachers provide opportunities for African American boys to read and discuss texts in an informal, nongraded, and interest-driven format. The African American boys who are involved in these programs determine the goals and objectives of the programs.

Weekly reading showcases—when teachers provide weekly opportunities for African American boys to share what they are reading with other students in the school in traditional and nontraditional formats, such as a television show, dramatic expression, song, and so on.

Schoolwide genre, theme, author, or illustrator studies—when teachers work with other school officials to identify genres, themes, authors, or illustrators for African American boys to explore collectively.

Practical Strategy 3: Invite and Involve Parents and Community Members

A third strategy that teachers can implement to make reading socially interactive is to involve and engage parents in the reading activities that occur in the classroom and across the whole school. While it is quite common for preK–5 teachers to encourage parents and community members to support reading activities at home, it is less common for teachers to involve parents and community members in the reading activities that happen at school.

African American boys are more likely to engage in reading when they are permitted and encouraged to explore books with significant adults in their lives (mom, dad, grandma, brother, coach, pastor, etc.). Consequently, teachers should strive to develop innovative ways of involving these individuals in the reading activities that happen at school. Some suggestions for involving family and community members in the reading activities that happen at school include but are not limited to:

Guest reader—teachers might encourage African American boys to identify a parent, guardian, sibling, relative, or community member to visit the classroom and read a text to the class.

Shared reading—African American boys might be encouraged to read a favorite text with a special person in the classroom.

Tutoring/enrichment—teachers might encourage African American boys to invite a special person to support and assist students in the classroom.

Literacy center facilitator—teachers might encourage family and community members of the African American boys in the classroom to oversee the literacy center activities in the classroom.

Text organizer—teachers might encourage family and community members of the African American boys in the classroom to assist in organizing text collections for specific purposes.

Project assistant—teachers might encourage family and community members of the African American boys in the classroom to assist students in the classroom while completing special reading projects.

Principle 6: African American Boys Should Receive Adequate Support While Reading

African American boys are likely to be more engaged during reading activities and tasks when teachers provide them with the tools, resources, and assistance necessary to be successful. For this reason, teachers should structure reading lessons in ways that provide extensive tools and support to African American boys all throughout the lesson. African American boys who feel successful while engaging in reading activities and tasks are likely to read more often than African American boys who frequently experience challenges and difficulties while reading.

Practical Strategy 1: Provide Support before Reading the Texts
Teachers should provide an extensive amount of support to African American boys before reading the texts to ensure that they are fully aware of important vocabulary, background information, authors' purposes, and so on. Some simple ways that teachers might provide support prior to reading texts include the following:

Teaching important vocabulary words explicitly—teachers might identify a few key vocabulary words to teach before reading the texts. This will allow African American boys to spend less time on identifying the meaning of key words while reading. This will also allow them to focus more of their attention toward other aspects of texts.

Activating prior knowledge—teachers might look for ways of making connections between what African American boys already know and what they will encounter in the texts.

Previewing the texts—teachers might give African American boys three minutes or less to preview the texts with a partner while jotting down anything that stands out to them. This will help them develop background knowledge before reading.

Introducing the characters in the texts before reading the texts—teachers might spend some time exploring the traits of key characters before reading the texts. This will help them develop background knowledge related to the characters.

Examine the illustrations in the texts—teachers might give African American boys three minutes or less to explore the illustrations in the texts while noting initial personal connections and interpretations.

Modeling/reviewing important reading strategies—teachers might teach specific problem-solving strategies that should be applied while reading the texts.

Practical Strategy 2: Provide Support While They Are Reading the Texts

Some ways that teachers might support African American boys while they are reading texts include the following:

Posing questions for clarification and elaboration purposes—teachers might pose a series of questions to check for understanding and to highlight key aspects of the texts while African American boys are reading.

Use sticky notes to document questions—teachers might pass out sticky notes and have African American boys write down questions that develop as they read.

Utilizing graphic organizers—teachers might incorporate graphic organizers and conceptual maps for African American boys to use to document key events and concepts in the texts.

Proving time to pause and reflect—teachers might pause periodically while reading aloud to provide time for African American boys to process and reflect on the content in the texts.

Integrate visual images to support concepts—teachers might provide additional images, photos, videos, or illustrations to support the content being presented in the texts that African American boys are reading.

Practical Strategy 3: Provide Support after They Finish Reading the Texts

Some ways that teachers might support African American boys after they finish reading texts include but are not limited to:

Summarizing events—teachers might encourage African American boys to summarize key events in the texts either orally or in writing.

Rereading for fluency practice—teachers might encourage African American boys to reread a text in a different manner to build fluency skills.

Visually representing story events—teachers might encourage African American boys to represent key events in the texts in a visual mode, such as poster, mural, painting, slide show, and so on.

Participating in a dramatic exercise—teachers might encourage African American boys to act out the events in the texts.

Discussing personal feelings and perspectives—teachers might encourage African American boys to discuss their personal feelings and perspectives on texts in small groups.

Principle 7: African American Boys Must Receive Feedback while Reading

Generally speaking, teachers can increase students' motivation to learn by providing frequent feedback about their progress (Hattie and Timperley 2007). With that said, African American boys who receive appropriate, immediate, and ongoing feedback from teachers during reading activities are more likely to be more engaged than African American boys who do not receive it. Teachers must keep the following characteristics in mind for this feedback to produce optimal results:

Time—teachers should provide feedback in a timely fashion. It should be immediate or shortly after a reading activity or task has been successfully completed.

Positivity—teachers should take special care to make sure that the feedback they give is framed in a way that builds up, as opposed to framing it in a way that tears down.

Consistency—teachers need to provide feedback regularly for it to produce significant results.

Clarity— teachers should provide African American boys with feedback that is based on clearly articulated outcomes and expectations. An easy way to achieve this goal is to incorporate rubrics into the reading activities that relate to academic and social expectations. Teachers should take some time at the beginning of each activity to make sure that the African American boys are fully aware of the outcomes and expectations they are working toward accomplishing while involved in the activity.

Brevity—teachers should provide feedback that is short and to the point. African American boys are more likely to respond to short and direct feedback than feedback that is elaborate and ambiguous.

Format—teachers should provide both formal and informal feedback throughout their reading lessons.

Practical Strategy 1: Incorporate Multiple Forms of Feedback

As mentioned all throughout this book, African American boys are not homogeneous. As a result, it is necessary to incorporate different forms of feedback during reading lessons. Teachers should use verbal, written, and symbolic forms of feedback throughout their reading lessons. Some examples of how teachers might provide written feedback to African American boys during reading lessons include the following:

Observation logs—teachers might observe African American boys while engaged in specific reading activities and tasks and use an observation log to note their performance. Teachers can then share these notes with the African American boys to provide immediate feedback related to their reading progress.

Exit slips—teachers might end their reading lessons by having the African American boys complete a brief formative assessment to document their learning. For example, after learning about adjectives, Ms. Turner might ask the African American boys with whom she is working in small groups to list on a sheet of paper three adjectives to describe their classroom.

Dialogue journals—teachers might encourage African American boys to document their learning in a journal that will be shared with and responded to by others in the classroom.

Checklists/rubrics—teachers can use checklists and rubrics to provide written feedback related to specific reading skills, such as fluency, accuracy, and word solving.

Teachers should keep the following recommendations in mind as they provide direct verbal feedback to African American boys in their classrooms:

Acknowledge effort—teachers should acknowledge or recognize the effort that was exerted even if the response is incorrect. For example, Ms. Turner might acknowledge effort by saying something like "I really like how Jamal is giving his all at the letter writing center!"

Acknowledge risk taking—teachers should acknowledge students who are making attempts at solving problems or answering questions that they normally would not answer. For example, Ms. Turner might say something like "I appreciate how Jamal was willing to sound out that very difficult vocabulary word!"

Acknowledge accurate responses—teachers should acknowledge or recognize responses that are correct. For example, Ms. Turner might say something like "Your response is correct, Jamal! The setting of the story is the forest."

Acknowledge ways of improving—teachers should provide verbal feedback related to ways or methods of improving performance. For example, Ms. Turner might say something like, "The next time you get to a word you don't know, remember to look for smaller words inside of the larger word."

Inasmuch as some African American boys will respond more often to written and verbal feedback, other African American boys will respond more often to visual feedback during reading lessons. As a result, teachers should also incorporate visual feedback into their reading lessons in an effort to increase reading engagement in African American boys. Some examples of visual feedback include but are not limited to:

Positive facial expressions—one simple and easy way that teachers can provide African American boys with positive visual feedback is to smile or provide some other affirming facial gesture.

Positive body movements—teachers can also provide African American boys with positive visual feedback through positive body movements, such as thumbs-up or high fives.

Visual representations of progress—teachers can also provide African American boys with positive visual feedback by using stickers, stamps, or graphs to represent reading performance and progress.

Practical Strategy 2: Vary the Source of the Feedback
In addition to providing direct feedback to African American boys, teachers should offer ways for African American boys to receive feedback about their reading performance and progress from other students in the classroom. Peer feedback is beneficial in two important ways. First, it lowers some of the anxiety commonly associated with receiving feedback from a teacher. As a result, the motivation to read and learn is inevitably increased. Next, peer feedback teaches African American boys how to listen and respond to the ideas of others in constructive ways.

Practical Strategy 3: Balance the Quantity and Quality of Feedback
Providing too much feedback during a lesson can leave African American boys feeling overwhelmed. At the same time, African American boys are likely to be paralyzed by predominantly negative feedback. Hence, teachers should make sure they are balancing the quantity and quality of feedback they give during a reading lesson.

As a suggestion, teachers should consider what is known as the "3–2–1 rule" relative to feedback. Teachers should begin by providing feedback about three academic skills or objectives that the African American boys successfully accomplished during the reading activity. Next, teachers should provide feedback about two social skills the African American boys successfully accomplished during the reading activity. Finally, the teacher might conclude this process by making one specific recommendation for improvement.

Principle 8: African American Boys Should Be Allowed to Interact with Technology while Reading

Most of today's learners live in technologically saturated worlds outside the classroom (Clarke 2005). With that said, it is likely that African American boys will become more engaged in reading activities if these activities involve technology. Some forms of technology that teachers might incorporate into reading lessons to increase reading engagement in African American boys include the following:

Audio Books

Instead of having the African American boys in her classroom read the text in a traditional manner, Ms. Turner might consider having them listen to the story on a CD as a means of increasing reading engagement.

Electronic Books

Ms. Turner might consider having the African American boys in her classroom read an interactive version of the text on an iPad, Kindle, or some other reader to increase reading engagement.

Multimedia Texts

Instead of reading social studies contents from the traditional hardback textbook, Ms. Turner might create an original multimedia version of the text to have the African American boys read and interact with it on the SMART board in her classroom. Ms. Turner's version might include additional sounds, images, video, and narration that the original textbook did not include.

Digital Games

Ms. Turner might find creative and innovative ways of incorporating excerpts from popular video games into her reading lessons with the African American boys. For example, after finding out that many of the African

American boys in her classroom enjoy playing *Super Mario Brothers* on their interactive video game systems at home, Ms. Turner might decide to incorporate images and content from this game into her daily oral language practice to increase engagement among these boys.

Information Communication Technologies

Ms. Turner might provide opportunities for the African American boys in her classroom to practice their reading skills using information communication technology tools. Some examples of the tools that she might use are

- Blogs
- Wikis
- Voice Thread
- Flickr
- Comic Life
- E-mail
- Games
- Kidpix
- Soundcloud

Popular Media

Ms. Turner might incorporate events, concepts, and characters from popular media in her lesson in an effort to increase reading engagement among African American boys in her classroom. For example, after learning that many of the African American boys in her classroom enjoy watching *Phineas and Ferb* on the Disney Channel each day after school, she might decide to incorporate content, ideas, and characters from this television show into her reading lessons.

Principle 9: African American Boys Should Read Texts from Real Life

African American males are more likely to engage in reading materials that connect to and are used in everyday life (Tatum 2006). Hence, in an effort to increase reading engagement in African American boys, teachers should strive to incorporate more opportunities to read texts that are seen and used in the homes and communities of African American boys. Some examples of real-life texts include:

- Local newspaper
- Restaurant menu

- Recipes
- Ingredients on food packages
- Signs at a grocery store
- Notes on the refrigerator at home
- Instructions for assembly
- Community signs
- Street signs
- Letters
- Lists
- Calendars

Practical Strategy 1: Learn from the Homes and Communities of African American Boys

It is impossible to develop a substantive knowledge base and understanding of the texts that are readily available in the homes and communities of African American boys by simply asking questions. Therefore, teachers should spend some time visiting the homes and communities of the African American boys in their classrooms as a means of learning firsthand the nature of the texts that are used on a daily basis outside school.

Teachers can accomplish this goal in three ways. First, they can visit the homes of the African American boys in their classrooms. Parents and teachers should negotiate mutually agreed-on dates and times for these visits. During these visits, teachers should make an effort to document the types of texts that are visibly being used in the home. They should also note the reason that each text is being used.

The second way that teachers can accomplish this goal is by conducting casual interviews with parents, guardians, and other significant community members of the African American boys in their classroom. This will give teachers another means of learning about the types of texts being used in their homes and communities on a regular basis.

The third way that teachers can learn from the homes and communities of African American boys is by serving in a volunteer capacity in the local communities of the African American boys in the classroom. For instance, Ms. Turner might decide to volunteer once per month at the local church where two of the boys in her classroom attend to learn more about the types of texts that are available for reading within this context. This will give Ms. Turner valuable information to use in her reading lessons at school.

Practical Strategy 2: Establish Connections between Texts
A second strategy that teachers can use to incorporate real-life texts in the classroom is to structure lessons in ways that allow students to make natural connections between texts used outside of school and texts used inside of school. For instance, let us suppose that Ms. Turner is teaching a lesson on goods and services. After learning about the types of texts that exist at a local restaurant that the African American boys in her classroom visit frequently, Ms. Turner might begin the lesson by passing out a copy of the menu for the boys to explore.

After giving the boys some time to explore the menu, she might then ask them to identify the object and its purpose and to read what it says. Immediately, the boys will recognize the menu and its source of origin. Ms. Turner might then establish a connection between the local restaurant and a text used in school related to "services" in the community. This type of building background activity is likely to motivate the boys to read more about goods and services in the classroom.

Principle 10: Teachers Must Establish High Expectations for African American Boys

There is a direct relationship between teachers' expectations and student performance in the classroom. Generally speaking, students often rise to the level of expectations that their teacher has set before them (Tyler and Boelter 2008). When it comes to reading performance and progress, teachers tend to have lower expectations for boys than for girls. In this same vein, many teachers expect African American boys to be struggling or low-achieving readers.

Unfortunately, teachers who hold low expectations often create and implement low-level reading activities that directly correspond with these low expectations. In many cases, these activities consist of nothing more than "drill and skill" remedial worksheets that do not hold the attention of African American boys. In an effort to reverse this trend, teachers should establish and maintain high expectations for this group.

Practical Strategy 1: Identify and Eliminate Stereotypes
Teachers must be willing to identify the stereotypes and misconceptions that they may hold toward African American boys and reading. After identifying these stereotypes and misconceptions, they must then be willing to confront

and overcome them. For instance, let us suppose that Ms. Turner decides to critically examine her belief systems and ideologies for unknown stereotypes and misconceptions. Through critical reflection, she realizes that she thinks girls are generally better readers than boys. She now has to be willing to eliminate these stereotypes to increase reading engagement in African Americans boys.

Practical Strategy 2: Communicate High Expectations for All African American Boys

A second way that teachers can counter the low expectations that often confront African American boys is to consistently communicate confidence and faith in their ability to read. Teachers should make a conscious and consistent effort to tell the African American boys in their classrooms that they believe in them and their reading abilities. Teachers should focus on communicating messages like "I think you can" or "You are an excellent reader" instead of messages like "I think you can't" or "You are not a good reader" to the African American boys in their classrooms.

Practical Strategy 3: Take Actions That Are Consistent with High Expectations

A third way that teachers can eliminate low expectations toward African American boys and reading is to take actions are consistent with high expectations. In other words, teachers must be willing to engage the African American boys in their classrooms in the same types and quality of reading activities, texts, and tasks that the high-achieving students in the classroom are engaged in on a regular basis. Teachers must make sure that the African American boys in their classrooms have access to the same quality and rigor in their reading lessons as the other students in the classroom.

Key Points to Remember

This chapter outlines ten principles for increasing reading engagement in African American boys in preK–5 contexts. To recap, some ways to increase reading engagement include but are not limited to:

- Considering the value and meaningfulness of texts
- Incorporating a variety of types of texts
- Providing multiple and ongoing reading opportunities
- Offering choice
- Creating reading opportunities that involve social interaction

- Giving support where needed
- Demonstrating ongoing and extensive feedback while reading
- Scheduling opportunities to read with and through technology
- Delivering opportunities to read real-life texts
- Establishing and maintaining high and positive expectations about reading and African American boys

Reflection and Discussion Questions

- Which one of the ten principles resonates most with you? Why?
- Which one of the ten principles do you agree with least? Why?
- What principle would you add to the existing list? Why?
- Select one of the practical strategies listed in this chapter. Discuss in detail how you might implement this strategy in your own context.

CHAPTER FOUR

Increasing Reading Achievement in African American Boys

As mentioned previously, the factors that contribute to reading disengagement and underachievement in African American boys span multiple social, cultural, and physical contexts. As a result, teachers must be willing to work within and across multiple contexts to increase reading outcomes for this group (figure 4.1). This chapter introduces and discusses a three-part framework for increasing reading achievement in African American boys. The first part involves strategies that teachers might implement within the curriculum.

The second part involves strategies that teachers might implement within in their classrooms. This section of the framework discusses how teachers might use various forms of assessment to better inform their instruction with African American boys. In addition, it presents examples of active and multisensory learning strategies that teachers might implement in their classrooms to increase reading outcomes in and among African American boys.

The third part of the framework involves strategies that teachers, administrators, literacy coaches, and other important school officials might implement across the entire school building to increase reading outcomes in and among African American boys. Strategies related to positive behavioral support and male reading mentoring programs are discussed. It is important to reiterate that "reading achievement" as referred to in this chapter and throughout the book is defined as measured reading outcomes related to phonics, phonemic awareness, fluency, comprehension, and vocabulary.

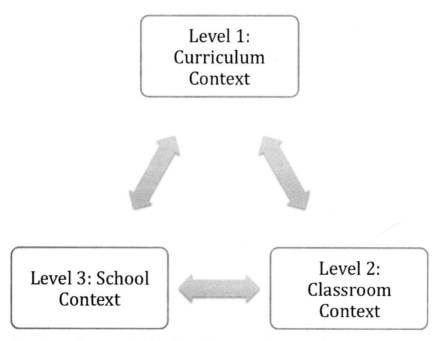

Figure 4.1. Three Levels within the Multi-Contextual Framework

Part 1: Curriculum Context

The first part of the three-part framework for increasing reading achievement in African American boys involves strategies that might be applied within the reading curriculum. Whenever feasible, teachers and school librarians should incorporate more texts in the reading curriculum that are consistent with the cultural backgrounds of African American boys. At the same time, teachers and school librarians should incorporate more informational texts within the reading curriculum.

Practical Strategy 1: Use More Culturally Consistent Literature
One strategy that teachers might implement to increase reading achievement in African American boys is to incorporate more culturally consistent literature in the reading curricula being used throughout the school. African American boys are more likely to grasp academic concepts when they are presented in ways that build on culturally situated ways of knowing, understanding, and communicating. In short, culturally consistent literature is literature that:

- Invites and involves students' social and cultural experiences
- Mirrors the day-to-day experiences of students from a particular social and cultural background
- Highlights the histories of students from a particular social and cultural background
- Accurately depicts the historical events and figures of students from a particular social and cultural background
- Honors and celebrates the cultural traditions of a particular group of students
- Consists of characters with authentic and relatable experiences
- Includes the language and communications styles of students from a particular social and cultural background
- Uses multiple genres to tell the story of a group of people from a particular social and cultural background

As teachers strive to incorporate more culturally consistent literature in the reading curriculum, they should keep in mind the following recommendations:

- Provide an extensive amount of variety.
- Display culturally consistent literature around the classroom to attract attention.
- Give African American boys opportunities within the curriculum to engage with these texts on a daily basis.
- Have African American boys read culturally consistent literature on a daily basis.
- Offer African American boys additional opportunities to explore culturally consistent texts beyond the initial learning experience.
- Provide scaffolding before, during, and after reading culturally consistent literature.
- Carefully evaluate the degree of cultural consistency of a text before incorporating it into the curriculum.
- Build connections between the language variations used in culturally consistent literature and the language used in formal schooling contexts.
- Assist African American boys in building connections between vocabulary presented in culturally consistent literature and the content-specific academic vocabulary presented in the school curriculum.

Practical Strategy 2: Use More Informational Texts

A second strategy that teachers should implement to increase reading achievement in African American boys is to incorporate more informational texts in the reading curriculum. As mentioned previously, boys tend to prefer to read informational texts more often than fiction texts. Therefore, teachers should use informational texts more often when teaching specific reading skills to African American boys. Some strategies that teachers might use with African American boys before reading informational texts include:

Making predictions—teachers might encourage African American boys to "take a walk" through the text and note important images, words, and pertinent information in the text to build background knowledge.

Previewing the features in the text—informational texts often have distinct features that fiction texts do not have, such as a table of contents, index, bold print, underlined print, photographs, diagrams, pictures, pronunciation key, maps, labels, chapter titles, headings, subheadings, and glossary. Teachers might encourage African American boys to preview these features before reading to build background knowledge.

Establishing a reading plan—teachers might encourage African American boys to develop a strategic plan for reading the text before actually reading it.

Developing focused initial questions—teachers might encourage African American boys to preview the text before reading and to develop a list of questions they plan to answer while reading.

Brainstorming—teachers might encourage African American boys to brainstorm the events and information that will be discussed in the text before reading the text.

Anticipation guide—teachers might create a guide with four to six statements for African American boys to agree or disagree with before reading a text. This will stimulate interest in the topic and set a purpose for reading.

Sorting words/concepts—teachers might encourage African American boys to sort key vocabulary words or concepts from the text into categories based on similar characteristics. Teachers can develop the categories in advance or have the African American boys develop the categories while they are involved in the activity.

Making connections—teachers might encourage African American boys to briefly scan the text and make connections between the photographs or bold material and their personal experiences.

Some strategies that teachers might use with African American boys during the informational text readings include:

Pause and pose—teachers might encourage African American boys to stop after reading each page and pose two questions for a partner to answer.

Graphic organizers—teachers might encourage African American boys to use various types of graphic organizers to represent knowledge, concepts, or ideas they acquire while reading the texts (appendix C).

Peer teaching—teachers might divide the texts into smaller portions and encourage African American boys to take turns teaching each part of the text to each other.

Concept mapping—teachers might encourage African American boys to develop diagrams to illustrate the relationship among various concepts in the texts.

Question generation—teachers might encourage African American boys to develop questions from a text for other students to answer while reading.

Concept matrix chart—teachers might encourage African American boys to use this chart to compare and contrast multiple dimensions of specific concepts in the text.

Sticky notes—teachers might encourage African American boys to note connections, questions, personal emotions, or unknown vocabulary while reading.

Coding the text—teachers might encourage African American boys to develop and implement a simple coding system to keep track of their thinking while reading.

Discussion web—teachers might present a controversial question from an informational text and encourage the African American boys to take a position and to include evidence on each spoke of the web as support.

Visualizing—teachers might encourage African American boys to develop mental images of concepts, events, and ideas presented in informational texts.

Some strategies that teachers might use with African American boys after they have read an informational text include

Identifying the text structure—teachers might encourage African American boys to identify the way in which the informational text is organized. The most common text structures include description, list, sequence, compare and contrast, cause and effect, and problem and solution.

Retelling—teachers might encourage African American boys to restate or explain the ideas from the text in their own words.

Summarizing—teachers might encourage African American boys to give the main ideas and details in a selection. Typically, summaries involve fewer details than retellings.

Distinguishing facts from opinions—teachers might encourage African American boys to identify the statements in the texts that can be proven true and the statements that are based on someone's judgments, beliefs, or opinions.

Identifying the author's viewpoint—teachers might encourage African American boys to identify the author's position on the information presented in the text.

Drawing conclusions—teachers might encourage African American boys to synthesize the details and information in a text in a way that produces larger claims or arguments.

Making generalizations—teachers might encourage African American boys to use the information presented in the texts to develop conclusions that can be applied to larger audiences or situations with similar characteristics.

Synthesizing new information—teachers might encourage African American boys to incorporate new information from a text into an existing knowledge base.

Recognize cause-and-effect relationships—teachers might encourage African American boys to identify what happened in a text and why.

Comparing and contrasting ideas—teachers might encourage African American boys to identify the connections that exist between known concepts and newly acquired concepts and information.

Sequencing events—teachers might encourage African American boys to identify the order of events in phases, cycles, or other developments in the texts.

Part 2: Classroom Context

The second part of the three-part framework for increasing reading achievement in African American boys involves strategies that teachers might implement within the classroom context. In short, these strategies pertain to issues of assessment and active and multisensory learning.

Practical Strategy 1: Use Multiple Assessments for Specific Purposes

Teachers often administer a variety of assessments in their classrooms to document students' learning and performance. In an effort to maximize reading achievement in African American boys, teachers should use reading assessments in three ways. First, teachers should use reading assessments to diagnose or identify the current needs, strengths, and interests of the African American boys they are serving. Diagnostic reading assessments should be given to determine the current level of knowledge and skill proficiency.

Teachers should use the information gained from these diagnostic assessments to make informed decisions related to what they will teach in the subsequent lessons. Information gained from these diagnostic assessments can also be used as a baseline or starting point to track the reading progress of African American boys over time. Some examples of diagnostic reading assessment include:

Informal reading inventories—assesses word recognition, word meaning, reading strategies, and comprehension

Qualitative reading inventories—use word lists and passages to assess oral and silent reading

Miscue analysis—allows teachers to analyze the errors that readers make while reading

In addition to using reading assessments to diagnose the current needs, strengths, and interests of the African American boys in the classroom, teachers should use reading assessments to monitor growth or changes in performance throughout the school year. Teachers should establish regular times throughout the school year when they will administer specific reading assessments to document the reading progress of African American boys over time. Some examples of reading assessments that teachers might use throughout the school year include

Dynamic Indicators of Basic Early Literacy Skills—a series of short fluency measures used to monitor the development of early reading skills

Peabody Picture Vocabulary Test—assesses expressive and receptive vocabulary knowledge and skills

Reading Fluency Progress Monitor—consists of fiction and nonfiction passages for teachers to use to analyze oral reading fluency regularly throughout the year

Teachers should also administer reading assessments to evaluate reading proficiency at a specific period. Some examples of reading assessments that teachers might use to evaluate reading proficiency in African American boys include:

> *National Assessment of Educational Progress*—standardized assessment measuring reading comprehension in the areas of literary experience, reading for information, and reading to complete tasks.
>
> *Benchmark Reading Assessments*—designed to measure student progress relative to short- and long-term goals.
>
> *End-of-Curriculum Unit Tests*—administered at the completion of a curriculum unit to measure students' knowledge related to contents presented in the unit. For example, after teaching a vocabulary unit on contractions, teachers might administer a unit test on this content.

Practical Strategy 2: Use Active and Multisensory Learning Strategies to Teach Reading

A second way that teachers can work toward increasing reading achievement in African American boys in the classroom is to implement active and multisensory learning strategies in their reading instruction. As mentioned earlier, African American boys are likely to be much more active than the girls. Teachers can respond to this activity by incorporating active and multisensory learning strategies during their reading lessons.

In short, active learning strategies place much more of the responsibility of learning on the learner than the teacher. Moreover, active learning strategies emphasize high levels of active engagement on the part of the learners involved. Essentially, active learning strategies encourage learners to move and do instead of sit passively for long periods.

Multisensory learning strategies focus on using more than one sensory mode (visual, auditory, tactile, and kinetic) to learn concepts, skills, and information (Gaines 2008). African American boys are more likely to benefit in instructional contexts where visual and other sensory-based learning is encouraged and supported than in classrooms where the primary mode of learning is auditory. Some ways that teachers might use active learning and multisensory strategies to teach specific reading skills in each of the five domains of reading are as follows:

Phonemic Awareness

Phoneme isolation. Phoneme isolation involves isolating the individual sounds in a word ("can" = /c/ is the first sound and /n/ is the last sound).

Teachers might teach this skill by engaging African American boys in games that focus on isolating individual sounds in words. A teacher might divide his or her students into pairs and have each boy take turns saying a word that begins with the same sound as the ending sound in the previous player's word. For example, one player may say "toast," and the next player will say "stop." "Toast" ends with the /st/ sound and "stop" begins with the /st/ sound.

Phoneme identification. Phoneme identification involves identifying the same sound in multiple words ("cat," "car," and "come" all begin with the /c/ sound). Teachers might actively teach this skill by displaying a series of picture cards in front of a small group of African American boys and having them match or identify the pictures that have the same beginning or ending phonemes.

Phoneme categorization. Phoneme categorization involves recognizing the word from a list that has different beginning or ending sounds ("go," "got," "run" = "run" does not fit because it does not have the /g/ sound). Teachers might actively teach this skill through an activity called "sort the treasure." During this activity, African American boys will be given a series of three photo cards. The teacher instructs them to examine the cards and deposit those that have the same initial sound in the treasure box. The card that does not have the same initial sound should be deposited in another container.

Phoneme substitution. Phoneme substitution involves substituting one phoneme for another to make a completely new word ("mug" becomes "bug" when you change the /m/ sound to a /b/ sound). Teachers might actively teach this skill through an activity called "trading sounds." During the activity, the teacher instructs the African American boys in the small group to begin by singing a well-known nursery rhyme, such as "Twinkle Twinkle Little Star." The teacher then instructs the boys to sing the song repeatedly while using a new phoneme each time.

Phoneme blending. Phoneme blending involves combining a sequence of phonemes to make a complete word (/c/a/t/ = "cat"). Teachers might actively teach this skill to African American boys by engaging them in an activity called "basketball blending." The teacher begins by saying the phonemes that make up a word individually. If one of the boys blends the phonemes into a word correctly, he will earn one point for his team. He will then be permitted to take a shot on the small basketball hoop. If the shot is made, this boy earns an additional point for his team.

Phoneme addition. Phoneme addition involves making a new word by adding a phoneme to an existing word (begin with the word "play" and add /s/ to the end to make "plays"). Teachers might actively teach this skill through an activity called "building words with blocks." The teacher begins by giving each African American boy in the small group three blocks. Each block has a letter on it. The teacher then instructs the boys to make the sound as he or she points to each block. Next the teacher asks one of the group members to select another block and read the new nonsense word.

Phoneme deletion. Phoneme deletion involves recognizing the new word after a phoneme has been removed ("mat" minus /m/ = "at"). Teachers might actively teach this skill by engaging African American boys in a small group activity called "bye-bye sound." The teacher will begin this activity by passing out an extra-large letter card to each African American boy in the group.

Then the teacher will have the boys line up in order to spell a short three- or four-letter word with their cards, such as "cat" or "play." When the teacher says "bye-bye sound," one of the boys is instructed to sit down. The other boys in the group are instructed to read the new word with the phoneme missing. For example, the boy with the letter "p" might sit down. The other boys are then instructed to read the new word, "lay."

Phoneme segmentation. Phoneme segmentation involves breaking a word into separate phonemes ("cat" = /c/ /a/ /t/). A teacher might actively teach this skill to African American boys through an activity called "play the phonemes." During this activity, each boy in the group is given a small toy instrument to play. The teacher displays a word card for the boys to view. When the teacher gives the signal, the boys will use the instruments to play a note that corresponds with each sound in the word. For example, if the teacher displays the word "cat," the boys will play three individual sounds that represent /c/ /a/ /t/.

Phonics

Consonants. Teachers might actively teach consonants to African American boys by engaging them in an activity called "consonant concentration." During this activity, the teacher displays a series of picture cards in front of each boy in the group. The boys are then instructed to select cards that have pictures that begin with the same sound. Teachers might consider using images from popular culture to make this activity relevant to the boys involved.

Vowels. Teachers might actively teach short or long vowel sounds to African American boys through an activity called "sort the sound." The teacher begins this activity by displaying two boxes before the boys in the group. One box has a label with the word "hot" attached to it. The other box has a label with the word "home" attached to it. Each boy in the group is given several counters.

The teacher reads a word from a list that has either a short or long "o" sound. If the boys think the word has a long vowel sound, they are instructed to place their counter in the box labeled "home," which represents the long "o" sound. If the boys think otherwise, they are instructed to place their counter in the opposite box.

Compound words. Teachers might actively teach compound words to African American boys by engaging them an activity called "compoundo." The teacher prepares for this activity by locating a series of large and oversized Lego blocks. The teacher should use only blocks that can attach themselves horizontally. The teacher should affix a label with one word on each block. The teacher provides clues and instructs the boys to take turns attaching the blocks that make a compound word that corresponds with each clue. The boys then record the new words and their definitions on a "compound chart."

Phonograms/word families. Teachers might actively teach phonograms and word families to African American boys by engaging them in an activity called "join the family." The teacher displays a can with a specific word family labeled on it, such as "at." The teacher also displays tiles with an onset labeled on each tile. Some of the tiles will make actual words if added to the word family; some of the tiles will not. The boys will toss each tile into the can while reading each newly constructed word.

Affixes. Teachers might actively teach affixes to African American boys by engaging them in an activity called "racing affixes." The teacher begins this activity by displaying a large chart with various root words listed. The teacher also displays large cards with a different suffix on each card. When the teacher says "go," the boys race to attach the suffixes in the correct spaces. The team that completes the chart fastest and with the correct responses is deemed the winner.

Syllabication. Teachers might actively teach syllabication to African American boys by engaging them in an activity called "syllable stomp." The teacher instructs the boys to stand and listen to a series of words that he or she will dictate. When the teacher gives the boys a signal, they all use their feet to stomp each syllable in the word. The boys then use their fingers to signal the number of syllables that exist in each word.

Comprehension

Metacognition. Teachers might actively teach metacognition to African American boys by engaging them in an activity called "what's going on in your brain?" During this activity, the teacher instructs the boys to read while listening for a timer to sound. When the timer sounds, the teacher calls on one of the boys to share the information he is thinking about at that exact moment. The other boys also share what they were thinking at that moment. After the discussion, the boys resume reading where they left off until the timer sounds again. The teacher should set the timer for two minutes each time.

Retelling/summarizing. Teachers might actively teach retelling and summarizing to African American boys by having them create a "newscast" of the events in the text. The teacher might use a camera phone and some form of video-editing software to create a clip of the students retelling key events within a text.

Literal comprehension. Teachers might actively teach literal comprehension to African American boys by having them create a cartoon that represents the events within the text.

Inferential comprehension. Teachers might actively teach inferential comprehension to African American boys by isolating a problem that exists within the text and having them dramatize or act out a solution to the problem.

Evaluative comprehension. Teachers might actively teach evaluative comprehension to African American boys by having them engage in a structured debate based on a position or perspective represented in the text. The teacher might assist each boy in writing his opening and closing arguments. The debate should last a minimum of three rounds. The teacher should serve as the judge and award one point to the winner of each round.

Fluency

Accuracy. Teachers might actively teach accuracy to African American boys by engaging them in an activity called "race to the end." For the purpose of this activity, the teacher displays a game board with high-frequency words written in a nonlinear fashion. When the teacher says "go," one player takes a toy car and drives it over each word while saying the word as fast as he can. If he reads the word incorrectly, the teacher says "go back," and the boy makes additional attempts at reading the word correctly. The teacher uses a timer to keep track of how long it takes each player to get from one side of the board to the other.

Speed. Teachers might actively teach speed to African American boys by creating "fluency cards" with words or short phrases for them to practice reading as quickly as they can. To make this activity more appealing and engaging, the teacher might include pictures from popular media that relate to the boys' personal interests.

Expression. Teachers might actively teach expression to African American boys by engaging them in an activity called "reader's reality." During this activity, the teacher will work with the boys in the group to create an original reader's theater script based on their personal lives and experiences. The teacher then assigns various parts in the script and instructs the boys to read each part at the appropriate time with expression.

Vocabulary

Application. Teachers might teach application by engaging African American boys in an activity called "vocabulary circles." The teacher instructs the boys to engage in a conversation while attempting to incorporate various robust or technical vocabulary words into the conversation. Each boy is given two vocabulary word cards to incorporate into the conversation.

Meaning. Teachers might actively teach meaning to African American boys by engaging in a vocabulary game known as "vocabulary charades." During this activity, the boys compete in teams and take turns acting out the meaning of vocabulary words from a word list.

Word knowledge. Teachers might actively teach word knowledge to African American boys by having them create original and visually rich dictionaries and thesauri of important technical and content-specific vocabulary.

Part 3: Comprehensive School Context

The third part of the multistrategic framework involves strategies that should be implemented across the entire school to increase reading achievement in African American boys. The two areas of focus within this part of the framework include positive behavioral support and alternative reading support systems.

Practical Strategy 1: Develop and Implement Schoolwide Positive Behavior Support Systems

As mentioned previously, many of the existing disciplinary policies in schools have led and continue to lead to disproportionate numbers of African American boys being removed from the classroom. This time spent away from the classroom frequently has a direct impact on reading development. In an effort to rectify this issue, schools should develop and implement positive behavioral support systems that focus on keeping African American boys in the classroom while addressing undesired behaviors.

For clarification purposes, a positive behavior support system is defined as a positive and proactive systemic initiative, intervention, or program that is implemented across an entire school context to increase desired behavior outcomes in a specific group of students (Sugai and Horner 2009). In other words, positive behavior support systems use positive and proactive actions to produce positive results in particular groups of students.

There are two key components involved in developing and implementing an effective positive behavior support system with African American boys: behavior modification and character/moral development (figure 4.2). Essentially, behavior modification involves applying consequences to manage, change, or shape specific behaviors over a period of time. Positive consequences used to strengthen desired behaviors—such as reading quietly during independent reading, fully engaging in a reading activity, and/or responding to questions orally—are known as "reinforcers."

Negative consequences that are applied to weaken unwanted behaviors—such as running around the classroom, being off task, or ignoring instructions—are known as "punishments." The fundamental goal within a positive behavior support system is for teachers, administrators, coaches, and other

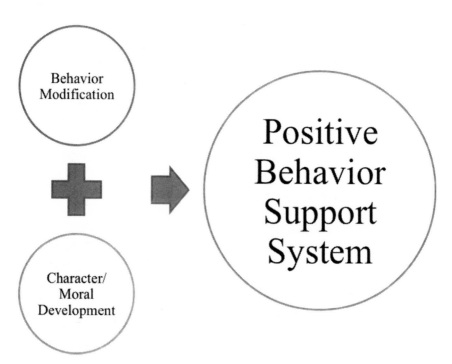

Figure 4.2. Components of Positive Behavior Support System

school officials to spend the majority of their time and energy on administering positive consequences to reinforce desired behaviors in a particular group of students. Some ways that teachers might reinforce desired behaviors in African American boys in a positive manner include:

Implementing proactive classroom management practices—when teachers and other school officials modify behavior through effective teaching practices, frequent and ongoing monitoring procedures, clearly stated rules and expectations, and consistent praise and feedback

Modeling prosocial behavior—when teachers and other school officials model desired ways of behaving and interacting in various schooling contexts, such as reading group and recess

Direct reinforcement—when teachers and other school officials implement various forms of positive reinforcement rewards, incentives, and programs to directly reinforce desired behaviors in the classroom and throughout the school

For reinforcers to be effective, they must be administered immediately after the targeted or desired behavior occurred. These reinforcers must also be administered on a consistent basis. Some examples of rewards, incentives, and programs that teachers might use to reinforce desired behaviors in African American boys are

- Verbal praise
- Token economy systems
- Free time on the computer
- Lunch with the teacher
- Stickers
- Award or trophy
- Visit to the school store
- "Student of the day" recognition

Unlike the behavior modification approach discussed earlier, a character/ moral development approach focuses on equipping African American boys with the tools, knowledge, and skills necessary to make appropriate behavior choices in the classroom and throughout the broader school context (Lintner 2001). Some strategies that teachers might develop and implement to contribute to the character and moral development in African American boys include:

Positive conflict resolution instruction—when teachers and other school officials work with African American boys to teach them how to respond to social conflict in ways that lead to positive outcomes for themselves and others

Effective communication outlets—when teachers and other school officials work to develop and implement clear and open channels of communication for African American boys to use when they are faced with social conflicts

Peer mediation circles—when teachers and other school officials equip and empower African American boys to handle their differences peaceably, without the use of formal disciplinary sanctions

Moral education—when teachers and other school officials explicitly teach African American boys how to "respect" the rights and differences of others in the classroom, school, and world around them

Practical Strategy 2: Develop and Implement Alternative Reading Support and Enrichment Programs

By and large, most of the reading programs that African American boys participate in at school focus on remediation. As such, African American boys have little, if any, extracurricular opportunities within the school to interact with texts in ways that focus on personal enjoyment or enrichment. In an effort to increase reading achievement in African American boys, teachers and other school officials should create and implement alternative reading support and enrichment programs that center on providing African American boys with meaningful, rich, and sustained interactions with texts. Some examples of alternative reading programs follow.

Reading Immersion Programs

Reading immersion programs are programs developed and implemented by teachers and other school officials wherein African American boys are encouraged to read as much as possible over specific periods of time. Participants are instructed to maintain some form of record of what they read between meetings. The participants then get together and discuss their responses to what they read. The fundamental goal of this program is to increase reading frequency.

Male Reading Role Model Programs

Male reading role model programs are developed and implemented by teachers and other school officials to connect African American boys with other African American males who enjoy reading. For the purposes of this program, each participant is matched with a male mentor to read and discuss various texts on a regular basis. The whole group meets periodically with their mentors to share what they are reading.

One major advantage of this program is that African American boys get an opportunity to witness other African American males reading and enjoying texts. Over the course of an extended period, African American boys then begin to see reading as more of a "guy thing" than something that is reserved exclusively for females.

Inquiry-Based Reading Programs

Developed and implemented by teachers and other school officials, inquiry-based reading programs center on reading real-world texts to find out about and potentially solve real-world issues. Participants begin by deciding on a real-world problem to explore and solve collectively. Then the teachers and school officials who are facilitating the program work with the participants to identify key texts related to this issue that they plan to read. After reading and discussing the specified texts, the participants work collectively to develop a real-world-based solution to the problem.

Key Points to Remember

This chapter discusses a three-part multistrategic framework for increasing reading achievement in African American boys. This framework outlines strategies for teacher, librarians, curriculum coaches, administrators, and other school officials to implement in and across the curriculum, classroom, and school. In short, the strategies mentioned in this chapter that relate to the curriculum context pertain to:

- Incorporating more culturally consistent literature
- Involving more informational texts
- Using multiple assessments for specific purposes
- Organizing active and multisensory learning activities
- Implementing positive behavior support systems
- Initiating alternative reading support programs
- Starting reading enrichment programs

Reflection and Discussion Questions

- Which part of the framework discussed in this chapter do you believe has the greatest influence? Why?

- Which of the strategies discussed in this chapter resonated most with you? Why?
- Which of the strategies discussed in this chapter do you believe will be the most difficult to implement in your context? Why?
- How might you adapt or amend the strategies discussed in this chapter to better meet the needs of African American boys in your context?

CHAPTER FIVE

Increasing Writing Engagement

Room 7: Ms. Brown's Fifth-Grade Classroom

Ms. Brown moves to the front of the classroom and waits for everyone's attention. Ms. Brown begins explaining the directions for the subsequent writing activity. "Okay, ladies and gentlemen, it is time for writing. Today we are going to be writing about a significant personal experience. Please take out your writing notebook and prepare to write at least five descriptive paragraphs on this topic. Also, remember to focus on your own work during writing time. I shouldn't hear any voices. You have about thirty minutes to complete this assignment. Are there any questions?"

The students remain quiet and look at Ms. Brown with blank stares. "Don't forget to check for periods, capital letters, grammar, and spelling," she warns. She continues, "I will be taking off points for every misspelled word and every sentence that is not written correctly! Does anyone have any questions?" The students remain quiet. "You may begin now."

The students begin working quietly on the assignment. After approximately twenty-seven minutes have passed, Ms. Brown announces to the class that the time allotted for the assignment is almost over. "This is your three-minute warning! You only have about three minutes left to finish the writing assignment. Please begin putting the finishing touches on your work." The students begin reading over their writing while checking for conventions. "Okay, ladies and gentlemen, time is up! Please pass your papers to the front of the room."

As Ms. Brown collects the papers, she notices that three of the African American boys in her classroom have turned in papers that have very few sentences written on them. She decides to deal with this situation by forcing the boys to make up their writing during recess time. Ms. Brown emphatically states, "I see that Ronald, Jamal, and Tommy have not finished their work. Therefore, you three gentlemen can see me during recess to finish your work!" The three boys look at each other with disappointment.

The events that transpire in this illustration are quite common in many elementary writing classrooms. Teachers often construct and facilitate classroom environments where African American boys are disengaged during periods of writing instruction. This chapter discusses ways of increasing writing engagement in African American boys.

For the purposes of this chapter, "writing engagement" is defined as the level of energy and effort that a student exerts during writing activities and tasks. It also refers to how frequently a student writes. With that said, this chapter begins by outlining and discussing some factors that contribute to writing disengagement in and among African American boys in preK–5 contexts:

- Variety
- Modeling
- Choice
- Feedback
- Social interaction
- Authenticity
- Hypercorrection
- Product approaches to writing instruction
- Digital technology
- Mentoring

Reading and writing are recursive processes (Graham and Hebert 2011). In other words, they tend to strengthen each other. Typically, a student's writing is positively influenced by the quantity and quality of texts he or she reads. At the same time, students often become better readers through participating in sustained and powerful writing activities. Hence, this chapter outlines ten practical strategies for increasing writing engagement in African American boys in preK–5 contexts. The underlying thought here is that by increasing writing engagement in African American boys, teachers will indirectly increase reading engagement in this group as well.

Factors That Contribute to Writing Disengagement

Generally speaking, boys tend to write less often than girls (Beard and Burrell 2010). Multiple factors contribute to writing disengagement in African American boys. Some are linked to issues associated with race, culture, and gender; others are linked to issues related to teaching and learning. While not exhaustive, these factors include the following:

Lack of Variety

Due to ever-increasing pressures for teachers to prepare students to perform well on standardized tests, many teachers emphasize teaching one genre of writing at the expense of teaching others (McCartney 2008). In many preK–5 classrooms, teachers focus almost exclusively on the type of writing that occurs on the yearly writing assessment measure (response to text, fiction narrative, etc.). In these classrooms, African American boys are often forced to write in genres that have little meaning and interest to them personally. Hence, writing becomes more a chore than a pleasure.

Lack of Models

Unfortunately, in many classrooms today writing is frequently assigned with little or no modeling involved. Teachers more or less provide students with a prompt and instruct them to write, without taking the time to explicitly model what an exemplary or excellent selection entails (Regan and Berkeley 2012). As such, many African American boys become less engaged during writing activities because they are unaware of the characteristics that are necessary to write an excellent selection.

Lack of Choice

In many elementary classrooms, teachers provide little choice over what students will write (Painter 2009). Essentially, teachers tell students what they will be writing about, as well as the parameters of the writing assignments. As with reading engagement, African American boys are likely to be more engaged in classroom settings where they have some input and choice into the nature of writing assignments than in classroom settings where they have little or no input into these matters.

Lack of Ongoing Feedback

In many elementary classrooms, students receive feedback on their writing only after the final draft has been submitted to the teacher (McGarrell and Verbeem 2007). In these classrooms, African American boys receive little or no feedback and encouragement along the way to keep them motivated and engaged during the writing process.

Lack of Social Interaction

As with reading, African American boys tend to be more engaged in writing activities that encourage social interaction than writing activities that focus on individual participation structures (Ghiso 2011). Many teachers facilitate writing lessons and environments that discourage peer interaction and communication. Unfortunately, these types of classroom environments often work to diminish writing engagement in African American boys.

Lack of Relevance

As with reading, African American boys tend to be more engaged in writing activities when these activities speak to their lived experiences, knowledge bases, and ways of communicating. Unfortunately, in many elementary classrooms, writing instruction often involves prompts and topics that have little or no relevance to the African American boys in the classroom (Collins 2006). As a result of this lack of relevance, many African American boys are disengaged and unmotivated during writing time.

Lack of Authenticity

Many teachers assign writing activities and assignments that have little or no real-life connection (Parsons and Ward 2011). In these classrooms, African American boys are required to write about topics and events that lack a real-world significance and audience. Consequently, many African American boys perceive writing to be an unimportant activity and process. Ultimately, this perception of writing has a negative impact on writing engagement in and among this group of students.

Overemphasis on Grammar and Conventions

In many classrooms, teachers place an overemphasis on the grammar and conventions that African American boys use in their writing. An overemphasis on grammar and conventions often impedes writing fluency and motivation (Sang-Keun 2008).

Focus on Product Approaches to Writing Instruction

Due to time constraints and standardized testing pressures, many teachers focus more on a product-oriented approach to writing instruction instead of a process-oriented approach (Karsbaek 2011). Essentially, the product approach to writing instruction provides little support to African American boys while they are completing a writing assignment. Consequently, many African American boys become discouraged and disengaged when they face writing challenges.

Writing Exclusively in Traditional Modes

Today's learners are highly influenced by digital and technological advances in society. Yet, many teachers continue to teach writing in ways that center primarily on traditional paper-and-pencil methods and modes. Because digital technology is such a reality in the everyday lives of so many African American boys, they often become disengaged when writing instruction has absolutely no connection with and to digital technology.

Lack of Culturally Situated Writing Mentors

Unfortunately, in many classrooms, African American boys do not have access to high-quality texts that are written by other African American males. As such, they often have difficulty identifying with writing as a social, cultural, or gendered activity. Essentially, due to a lack of exposure to other African American male authors, many African American boys see writing as something that is designated for girls, whites, and others.

Practical Strategies for Increasing Writing Engagement

Practical Strategy 1: Intentionally Vary the Nature of Writing Assignments

One practical strategy that teachers can use to increase writing engagement in African American boys is to intentionally and systematically vary the types of writing they assign in the classroom. The more the teachers vary the types of writing assigned, the greater the likelihood they are providing opportunities for African American boys to write in a genre they feel most comfortable. The seven most common types of writing that teachers should include in their instructional rotation in the classroom include the following:

> *Creative/expressive*—creative or expressive writing is anything that is written with the primary purpose of expressing thoughts, emotions, and feelings. Some examples that teachers might use in the classroom with African American boys are poetry, personal memoir, dramatic script, and journal entries.
>
> *Narratives*—narrative writing tells a fictional or nonfictional story. For example, teachers might encourage African American boys to write about specific personal experiences or events in their lives.

Expository/informational—the purpose of expository or informational writing is to explain or share information. For example, teachers might encourage African American boys to write an information report about their favorite hip-hop artist.

Descriptive—the purpose of descriptive writing is to describe a person, place, or event in a way that forms vivid images in the reader's mind. For example, teachers might encourage African American boys to write a description of their favorite video game or television show.

Persuasive—the purpose of persuasive writing is to convince the reader to agree with the author's point of view. For example, teachers might encourage African American boys to write an essay that persuades readers to watch a particular movie or television show.

Technical—the purpose of technical writing is to instruct a reader on how to do something. For example, teachers might encourage African American boys to explain in writing the directions to their favorite sport or video game.

Communicative—the purpose of communicative writing is to exchange personal thoughts and feelings between two people. For example, teachers might encourage African American boys to write a letter to their favorite children's literature author.

Response to text—the purpose of a textual response is to write about a specific aspect of a text in ways that demonstrate sufficient knowledge and understanding. An excellent written response typically involves a clearly stated opinion, evidence to support, personal connections, and personal conclusions.

Practical Strategy 2: Use Multiple Models

Another practical strategy that teachers can use to increase writing engagement in African American boys is to provide a number of models for them to refer to while they are in the process of completing a specific writing activity or task. African American boys who are equipped with high-quality models to refer to during the writing process tend to write more fluently than do students without. This is especially true when African American boys are asked to write in ways or genres of which they have little prior knowledge and experience.

In addition to providing teacher-generated models for African American boys to refer to and draw from during writing activities and tasks, teachers should provide models that are generated by other peers in the classroom. African American boys stand to benefit greatly from studying the elements of selections written by other students who share the same academic, social, cultural, and developmental spaces.

Whenever feasible, teachers should use models from writers who share the same social and cultural backgrounds of the African American boys in the classroom. For example, if Ms. Brown discovers that many of the African American boys in her classroom enjoy sports, she should look for peer models who incorporate sports in some form or fashion in their writing.

Practical Strategy 3: Provide Extensive Choice in Writing Activities and Tasks

Another strategy that teachers might use to increase writing engagement in African American boys is to allow them to choose (from a list of various options) the writing assignments they will complete in the classroom. African American boys who are given some degree of choice in what they write tend to write more extensively than do African American boys who are forced to write according to specific and narrow prompts, activities, or tasks. Hence, providing more options in writing activities and tasks will directly increase writing engagement in this group.

In like manner, teachers should allow African American boys to choose (from a list of various options) the ways in which their writing activities and tasks will be assessed. Teachers should collaborate with the African American boys in the classroom to co-construct the rubrics or assessment measures that will be used to assess various elements of their writing. Again, African American boys are more likely to attend to various traits on the rubric while writing if they had some input into deciding whether they should be there.

Practical Strategy 4: Provide Ongoing Feedback throughout the Writing Process

Another strategy that teachers might use to increase writing engagement in African American boys is to structure writing activities and tasks in ways that provide opportunities for them to give and receive ongoing feedback before completing the final draft. African American boys are likely to put more effort and energy into their writing in classroom contexts where they receive ongoing feedback from their teacher and peers than when they are in classrooms where they do not receive such feedback.

As a cautionary note, teachers may have to teach the African American boys how to give and receive appropriate and meaningful feedback. Without explicit instruction in this area, many of the boys may place an overemphasis on conventions and spelling instead of other key areas, such as voice, organization, sentence fluency, and so on.

Practical Strategy 5: Make Writing Social
Another strategy that teachers might use to increase writing engagement in African American boys is to make writing social. In other words, teachers can increase writing engagement by structuring activities and tasks in ways that require social interaction and collaboration. Teachers can make writing social in and among African American boys in their classrooms in the following three ways:

> *Writing collaboratively*—when teachers encourage African American boys to work with other African American boys during all phases of the writing process. For example, Ms. Brown might encourage the African American boys in her classroom to work in pairs to write a fictional narrative.
>
> *Writing for special audiences*—when teachers encourage African American boys to share their writing with special audiences, such as parents, teachers, and coaches. For example, Ms. Brown might encourage the African American boys in her classroom to share their writing with the other fifth graders during a grade-level "writer's showcase."
>
> *Write beyond the school*—when teachers encourage African American boys to share their writing beyond the walls of the school building using traditional and nontraditional means and modes. For example, after her social studies class writes letters to its local elected officials, Ms. Brown and her students might take a field trip to the city hall, and she might encourage the African American boys to share their letters with the elected officials in person.

Practical Strategy 6: Make Writing Activities and Tasks Relevant
Another strategy that teachers might implement to increase reading engagement in African American boys is to make the writing activities and tasks relevant to their life experiences. African American boys are more likely to engage in writing activities and tasks that value and reflect their personal experiences and perspectives than those that silence them. Whenever feasible, teachers should strive to implement writing activities and tasks that value and highlight the experiences, knowledge bases, and communication styles of African American boys.

Teachers should also consider making the writing activities and tasks relevant to the popular culture interests of African American boys. As mentioned earlier, today's learners spend a tremendous amount of time each week interacting with various forms of media and technology. Teachers can increase writing engagement in African American boys by incorporating some of this content into their writing activities and tasks.

While teaching African American boys how to write a response to a text, Ms. Brown might increase writing engagement by encouraging the African American boys in her classroom to write a response to a newly released television show on the Disney Channel. Again, African American boys are more likely to be engaged in writing activities and tasks that connect to their social interests outside the classroom than those that do not relate to their interests.

Practical Strategy 7: Write for "Real" Purposes and Audiences

Another strategy that teachers might use to increase writing engagement in African American boys is to develop and implement "real" writing activities and tasks for "real" purposes and audiences. Much like other student groups, African American boys tend to be more engaged in writing activities and tasks when these activities and tasks are connected to the real world and the people therein. Some ways that teachers might encourage and facilitate writing for real purposes and audiences include the following:

> *Enlisting coauthorship in everyday writing activities and tasks*—teachers might encourage African American boys to participate in the types of writing activities and tasks that happen naturally at school, such as constructing a to-do list, composing the morning message, making classroom rules, writing the instructions for a learning center, and so on.
>
> *Writing to discover/inquire*—when teachers encourage African American boys to use writing as a tool for learning and reflection. Instead of learning to write, this process involves using writing activities and tasks to learn more about a particular topic, idea, or theme.
>
> *Write for social change*—when teachers encourage African American boys to use writing as a means of identifying, resisting, and combating social injustices in society. For example, after teaching about the social injustices associated with racism, Ms. Brown might encourage the African American boys to write a letter to the government to respond to this issue.

Practical Strategy 8: Implement a Process-Oriented Approach to Writing Instruction

Another strategy that teachers might use to increase writing engagement in African American boys is to implement a process-oriented approach to writing instruction. Generally speaking, students tend to write more often and more extensively in classrooms that emphasize process-oriented approaches to writing instruction than in classrooms that focus on product-oriented approaches. The steps involved in a process-oriented approach to writing instruction are as follows:

Prewriting—involves thinking and deciding on a topic to write about. During this step, students typically brainstorm ideas about a potential writing topic, conduct research, and generate a list of possible writing ideas. Students are encouraged to share their ideas to receive feedback from peers and the teacher.

Drafting—involves constructing an initial draft based on the ideas generated during the first step. Students are encouraged to share their ideas to receive feedback from peers and the teacher.

Revising—when students work toward improving the quality of their initial draft. Students are encouraged to share their ideas to receive feedback from peers and the teacher.

Editing—when students work to check their writing for errors in grammar, spelling, capitalization, and so on. Students are encouraged to share their ideas to receive feedback from peers and the teacher.

Publishing—involves presenting the writing in a way that can be shared with an audience in the classroom, school, or community.

Practical Strategy 9: Write in Digital Modes with Digital Tools

Another strategy that teachers might use to increase writing engagement in African American boys is to provide opportunities for them to write in digital models. Again, many African American boys are used to interacting with a variety of digital technologies outside the classroom. Yet, they are afforded few opportunities to write in digital modes in the classroom. African American boys are more likely to be engaged in writing classrooms that incorporate digital writing opportunities than in classrooms that include only traditional writing opportunities. Some examples of digital writing tools that teachers might use to increase writing engagement in African American boys include the following:

Animoto—allows users to create presentations with their own images and music or from stock files

Audacity—a multilingual audio editor and recorder

Blabberize—a tool that allows users to create talking pictures

Comic Strip Creator—a digital comic strip creation tool

Creately—a tool that allows users to create diagrams online

Dipity—an interactive visual timeline tool

Edublogs—an educational blog created for teachers and students that is used in collaboration, reflection, and other school-related purposes.

Google Blogger—a blog-publishing service that allows private or multiuse blogs

Google Docs—a web-based word processor, spreadsheet, presentation, form, and data storage service offered by Google

iBooks—an application that allows users to create multitouch textbooks

iMovie—a video-editing software application

Infogr.am—a tool that allows users to create and display data in a visually engaging manner

Meograph—a four-dimensional storytelling tool

Movie Maker—video-editing software by Microsoft

Penzu—a tool that provides users with a realistic-looking journal

Photobucket—a website that allows users to store and share images and videos

Photostory—a Microsoft application that allows users to create a presentation using digital images

PicLit—a creative-writing site that connects images with words

Pinterest—a "virtual pinboard" that allows users to share images and engage in social networking

Podcast—a multimedia digital file that is made available for downloading to a portable media player or computer

PodOmatic—a tool that allows users to create their own podcasts

Popplet—a collective brainstorming tool that allows users to match images with text

PowerPoint—a presentation program by Microsoft

Prezi—a web-based presentation application and storytelling tool that uses a canvas instead of slides

Primary Pad—a web-based word processor designed for teachers and students to write together in real time

Screencast-O-Matic—an online screen recorder

SlideRocket—an online presentation tool

SMART Board—an interactive whiteboard developed by SMART Technologies

Sploder—an online game creator

StoryBird—a visual storytelling community

Text2Mindmap—a mind map that allows users to collaborate and share digitally

Toondoo—a comic creation website

Twitter—a social networking tool

VoiceThread—an online video collaboration tool

Voki—an educational tool that allows users to create their own character

Wikispaces—a tool for making custom webpages that students can edit together

Wordle—a tool for generating "word clouds" from text provided by the user

Zeen—a digital magazine–publishing tool

Zimmertwins—a website that invites students to share their digitally narrated stories

Practical Strategy 10: Develop and Implement Writing Programs That Connect African American Boys with African American Male Authors

Another strategy that teachers might use to increase writing engagement in African American boys is to develop and implement writing programs that connect African American boys with other African American male authors. For many African American boys in preK–5 contexts, writing is viewed as an activity reserved primarily for girls and whites. Many African American boys rarely come into contact with other African American male authors. As a result, they have difficulty identifying with writing as a social and culturally significant activity.

Teachers might work toward solving this issue in two ways. First, they should solicit older African American male authors to serve as "writing mentors" for younger African American boys. These writing mentors might be other African American males from middle school, high school, or collegiate contexts who are willing to share their academic, social, and personal writings with other African American boys in preK–5 contexts.

The second way that teachers can facilitate this writing mentorship process is by soliciting other African American male authors in the surrounding local, state, and regional contexts to serve as writing members for African American boys in preK–5 contexts. Essentially, these mentors would be asked to share their writing with African American boys in the school on a monthly, quarterly, or biannual basis. If possible, these mentors might also host a writing workshop for African American boys in a particular school or region.

Key Points to Remember

This chapter identifies several reasons why many African American boys in preK–5 contexts are disengaged during writing activities and tasks. This chapter also outlines several strategies that teachers might implement to respond to this issue. Some strategies to increase writing engagement in African American boys include:

- Incorporating variety
- Providing extensive modeling
- Offering choice
- Giving feedback
- Encouraging social interaction
- Delivering authentic writing opportunities
- Avoiding hypercorrection
- Implementing a process approach to writing instruction
- Including digital technologies and tools
- Enlisting writing mentors

Reflection and Discussion Questions

- Which one of the factors discussed in this chapter is most relevant in your context? Why?
- What additional factors might contribute to writing disengagement among African American boys in your context? Why?
- Which strategy do you believe is most significant for teachers to consider? Why?
- What other strategies might teachers consider to increase writing engagement in African American boys?

~

CHAPTER SIX

Partnering with
Parents and Guardians

It is nearly impossible to make significant and sustained gains in reading outcomes in and among African American boys without the ongoing energies and efforts of parents and guardians. Hence, this chapter outlines and discusses important ways that teachers might work with parents and community members to increase reading engagement and achievement in this group. The questions examined in this chapter are as follows:

- What are common reasons why some parents/guardians of African American boys are less involved than parents of other student groups in the reading activities at school?
- What are common reasons why some parents/guardians of African American boys are less involved than parents of other student groups in supporting and reinforcing reading practices at home?
- What are some strategies that parents/guardians of African American boys can implement outside of school to increase reading engagement and achievement in African American boys?
- What are some strategies that teachers can implement in their classrooms to encourage more parental and community support and involvement in the classroom?

Note that the homes and communities where African American boys live are not homogeneous. Some African American boys live in homes and communities where parents and guardians consistently support and reinforce the reading practices that occur in schools. At the same time, unfortunately, there are African American boys who live in homes and communities that offer very little reading support and reinforcement.

This chapter is not meant to vilify the latter group of parents and guardians in any form or fashion. After all, there is a myriad of reasons (social, institutional, political, cultural, etc.) why parents and guardians may not be able to fully support the reading practices that African American boys acquire at school, at home, and in their respective communities. Instead, this chapter intends to offer strategies for parents and guardians to use to better support the reading practices that occur in schooling contexts.

Reasons for Lack of Involvement and Support at School

There are multiple reasons why some parents and guardians of African American boys are minimally involved in supporting and reinforcing reading practices at school.

Lack of Confidence

One explanation why some parents of African American boys are minimally involved in supporting and reinforcing the reading practices that happen at school is that they lack confidence in their ability to make significant contributions in the classroom (Williams and Sánchez 2013). Many parents of African American boys see the teacher as the only "expert" in the classroom and themselves as having little or nothing of value to contribute to the students. Thus, many parents of African American boys are reluctant to volunteer their time and energy at school.

Low Expectations

In many classrooms, teachers only solicit parental involvement to assist in nonacademic tasks, such as party planning, field trip supervision, field day organizing, and so on. Many parents of African American boys are rarely invited to assist in the reading practices that occur within the classroom by their sons' teachers. Hence, parents of African American boys are often apprehensive about visiting the classroom without first receiving a formal invite to do so.

Scheduling Conflicts

Another reason why some parents of African American boys are less involved than the parents of other student groups in supporting and reinforcing the reading practices that happen at school concerns scheduling conflicts (Cooper and Crosnoe 2007). Most parental involvement opportunities offered at most schools typically occur during regular school hours. As a result, working parents often have a limited ability to participate at school without sacrificing time and money from work.

Social Climate

Many African American parents often report experiencing indifferent, resistant, and even hostile interactions with officials while visiting their children's schools (Jaleel and David 2006). Because of such negative experiences, many parents of African American boys are often reluctant about volunteering their expertise and services within the classroom and the broader school community.

Lack of Teacher Training

Another reason why some parents of African American boys are less involved in the reading practices that occur at school is that many teachers have not been adequately trained on how to engage parents in the classroom in effective and substantial ways. As a result of this lack of training, many teachers are reluctant to invite parents to assist in reading-related academic tasks in the classroom.

Reasons for Lack of Support and Reinforcement at Home

Inasmuch as there are multiple reasons why some parents of African American boys are less involved in supporting and reinforcing the reading practices that happen at school, there are multiple reasons why some parents of African American boys are less involved in supporting and reinforcing the reading practices of African American boys at home.

Different Expectations for Sons and Daughters

Many parents believe that girls are more inclined than boys toward reading and writing and other academic endeavors. These differences in expectations between girls and boys often play out in the amount of support that parents give to their sons and daughters during reading and writing activities at home.

Lack of Knowledge and Training

Many teachers take for granted that parents know how to support reading instruction at home effectively. While many parents are able to support reading instruction at home in broad and general ways, few are aware of specific strategies to use to support these skills at home. Lack of extensive knowledge and training in these areas often leads to inactivity on the part of many parents of African American boys.

Lack of Resources

Another reason why some parents of African American boys are less involved in supporting and reinforcing the reading practices of African American boys at home is that they lack the adequate resources to do so in substantive ways. Most parents do not have access to the same educational and technological resources that teachers use in the classroom. Consequently, parents often have difficulty mirroring what happens in the classroom at home.

Lack of Support

By and large, parents tend to be more involved and engaged in schools where dynamic communities of parental involvement exist than in schools where these communities do not exist. In other words, parents tend to be more involved and engaged when they feel supported by other groups of parents than in schools where they feel isolated or alienated. This lack of support can directly affect how involved parents of African American boys are in supporting the reading activities that happen at school at home.

Time Commitments and Constraints

Another reason why some parents of African American boys are less involved in supporting at home the reading activities that happen at school is that they are often faced with a myriad of commitments and constraints in their daily lives. Due to numerous reasons, many parents of African American boys are faced with responsibilities to fulfill at home that make it difficult for them to support the reading practices that happen at school.

Encouraging and Supporting Parental Involvement at School

As mentioned earlier, parents play an important role in helping African American boys become successful readers. There are several strategies that teachers should consider implementing at school to increase parental involvement in and among the parents of African American boys.

Communicating with Parents Using a Variety of Means

Many teachers today still communicate with parents using traditional modes and methods only, which produce minimal results. In an effort to increase parental involvement in the classroom, teachers should also consider communicating with parents using twenty-first-century information communication tools, such as Skype, Google Talk, e-mail, blogs, Facebook, and Twitter.

Designating Permanent Space in the Classroom and School for Parents

Another way that teachers might increase parental involvement in and among the parents of African American boys is to create designated spaces within the classroom and school for parents. Parents of African American boys who feel welcomed within the classroom and school environments are likely to volunteer more consistently than parents who feel unwelcomed.

Avoiding Judgmental Communication

Another way for teachers to increase parental involvement in the classroom and school environments is to avoid judgmental looks and comments. Parents of African American boys are often greeted with judgmental scowls, gestures, and words as they attempt to interact with various school officials. In an effort to increase parental involvement, teachers much become cognizant of these negative communication patterns and work toward replacing them with positive communication patterns.

Building Programs around Parents

Another way that teachers can work toward increasing parental involvement among the parents of African American boys is to structure parent programs in ways that take the interests, needs, and strengths of parents into consideration. A relatively simple way to find out the specific interests, needs, and strengths of the parents in a particular classroom is to conduct parental surveys or interviews at the beginning of the school year.

Recognize and Reward Parental Involvement

Another strategy that teachers might implement to increase parental involvement is to find ways to recognize and reward parental involvement in the classroom and throughout the school. Parents who are recognized and rewarded for their efforts tend to volunteer their expertise and services more often than parents who are not.

Phonemic Awareness Strategies
• Sing alphabet songs with their child • Read aloud stories • Clap the syllables in words • Identify letters in common words • Identify letters in your son's name • Read and sing language rhymes • Sing songs that teach phonemes like The Name Game
Phonics Strategies
• Help your son sort words by long and short vowel sounds, • Help your son define larger words by breaking them into smaller chunks • Play spelling and word games like Scrabble and Hang Man. • Ask your son's teacher about his phonics progress • Have your son point to words and same them out loud while writing
Fluency Strategies
• Read aloud often • Encourage your son to read aloud • Encourage your son to reread his favorite books • Model reading for multiple purposes • Act out events in a story or book • Read in multiple ways (i.e., echo, choral, etc.)
Vocabulary Strategies
• Read a variety of different genres with your son • Discuss books with your son • Discuss daily events with your son • Discuss how the illustrations and the text relate to each other in books • Find and define new words in the dictionary • Assist your son in developing new vocabulary based on their personal interests and hobbies

Figure 6.1.   Specific Strategies For Parents

Comprehension Strategies

- Ask your son to predict what will happen next in the story
- Ask your son who, what, when, where, and why questions while reading
- Ask your son to make personal connections while reading
- Ask your son to identify the main idea in a book
- Ask your son to recall events that occurred in the beginning, middle, and end of the story

Print Concept Strategies

- Point out the title and author's name to your son while reading together
- Talk to your son about where reading begins on the page
- Show him how the words flow left to right
- Play games to match lowercase and uppercase letters
- Expose your son to many types of print
- Make a book with your son using large print and illustrations

Writing Strategies

- Encourage you son to write letters to family members
- Model writing for different purposes
- Plan a consistent time each day and each week to write with your son
- Use writing to communicate with your son periodically
- Ask your son to say words out loud as he writes

Reading Interest Strategies

- Visit the bookstore or library at least once per week as a family
- Discuss books and or stories each day as a family
- Model reading for enjoyment regularly
- Give books and other texts as gifts

Encouraging and Supporting
Parental Involvement outside of School

Provide Models of Effective Instructional Strategies

One way that teachers can help support parents of African American boys at home is by providing models of effective reading strategies. Teachers should consider using various video-recording software to model specific reading strategies for parents to implement so that they can support reading achievement and engagement at home. These video recordings should provide opportunities for teachers to demonstrate specific strategies for parents to implement with their sons while reading.

Create a Parent Library of Teaching Resources and Materials

Another way that teachers can support parental involvement in the reading practices and activities that happen at home is by making a library of teaching resources available within the school for parents of African American boys to use at home with their sons. Some examples of the resources and materials that might be included in this library are curriculum manuals, decodable books, letter tiles, and picture cards.

Offer Ongoing Education, Training, and
Support Opportunities for Parents

Another strategy that teachers can use to better support parental involvement at home is to offer ongoing education, training, and support to parents on topics related to reading development. These training and support opportunities might assume three formats: one-hour general workshops, four-hour focused workshops, and two-day intensive summer institutes.

Solicit Community Participation and Partnerships

As mentioned, parents are often overwhelmed with the various responsibilities and commitments that detract from the time that they are able to spend supporting reading practices and activities at home with their sons. Teachers can help with these challenges by providing parents with a network of community volunteers or programs that are willing and available to provide support to African American boys related to their reading development.

Provide Specific Strategies in Each of the Five Areas

Another way that teachers can better support parent involvement outside of school is to provide specific and concrete strategies for parents to implement in each of the five areas of reading instruction discussed throughout this book. Parents of African American boys who have been made aware of specific and concrete ways of supporting their sons' reading development at home are more likely to be involved outside of school than parents who have not been made aware of strategies to help their sons succeed in reading (figure 6.1).

Key Points to Remember

This chapter explores multiple reasons why some parents of African American boys are less involved in supporting reading practices and activities at school and outside of school. This chapter also presents multiple strategies that teachers might apply to better support parental involvement in school and out of school. In short, some strategies that teachers can use to support parental involvement inside and outside of school include:

- Communicating with parents using multiple means and modes
- Creating designated spaces within the classroom and school for parents
- Avoiding passing judgment
- Initiating programs that respond to parents' specific needs, interests, and strengths
- Rewarding and recognizing parental effort and support throughout the school
- Providing parents with models of practices and strategies
- Offering parents access to teaching resources to support reading at home
- Giving opportunities for ongoing parent education and training
- Soliciting the efforts and initiatives of community volunteers and programs
- Identifying specific and concrete strategies that parents should implement at home

Reflection and Discussion Questions

- Of the reasons why some parents of African American boys are minimally involved at school, which is most significant in your context? Why?
- Of the reasons why some parents of African American boys are minimally involved at school, which is least significant in your context? Why?
- Of the strategies discussed in this chapter, which do you believe is most important for teachers to implement? Why?
- Identify at least one additional strategy that teachers might implement to increase parental involvement in reading practices outside of school.

~

Afterword

Today's information- and technology-based society requires its members to be fluent readers across various modes and mediums. With that said, not learning to read will have a detrimental impact on the economic, political, and social success of African American boys for many years to come. This book discusses principles and practices to aid teachers, administrators, literacy coaches, and parents in helping African American boys become fluent readers and lifelong lovers of texts. For these practices and principles to be effective, those who serve African American boys must first be willing to make three important changes.

First, individuals who serve African American boys must be willing to change the way they think about African American boys and their reading development. Parents and school officials must develop a willingness to do whatever it requires to ensure that all African American boys become avid readers and writers in society. No longer can parents and other school officials accept the reading achievement statuses of African American boys as a "normal" part of life.

Next, parents and school officials must be willing to change how they work toward increasing reading engagement and achievement in African American boys. These individuals must be willing to work collectively and collaboratively toward implementing the strategies presented in this book. Parents and school officials must be willing to work within and across the traditional boundaries of home, school, and classroom to improve reading outcomes in this group. Parents and school officials must begin to see this issue as something that affects all of us in equally powerful ways.

Finally, parents and school officials must be willing to constantly change what they know about African American boys. Parents and other school officials must commit to observing and interviewing African American boys on a consistent basis to gather information regarding their ever-changing interests, needs, and strengths. They must continue to learn about and from African American boys on a consistent basis and use this information to better inform their practices. This will allow parents and school officials to keep African American boys at the forefront of their decision-making processes instead of as an afterthought. Furthermore, failure to embrace these three calls may lead to similar or even worse reading outcomes in and among African American boys as we journey through the remainder of the twenty-first century.

Appendix A: Sample Texts with African American Males as Main Characters

Theme: History

Levinson, C. 2012. *We've Got a Job: The 1963 Birmingham Children's March*. Atlanta: Peachtree.

This book tells the experiences of children who were involved in the famous Birmingham march.

Micklos, J. 2008. *African American and American Indians Fighting in the Revolutionary War*. NJ: Enslow Elementary.

This book documents the experiences of African American and American Indian soldiers who fought in the Revolutionary War.

Pinkney, A., and B. Pinkney. 2010. *Sit-In: How Four Friends Stood Up by Sitting Down*. New York: Little, Brown Books for Young Readers.

This book documents the experiences of four African American college students who were involved in the historic sit-in at a Woolworth lunch counter in Greensboro, North Carolina.

Theme: Sports

Carlisle, B. 2009. *Overcoming Adversity: Sharing the American Dream*. Broomall, PA: Mason Crest.

This book shares major events in the life of championship football coach Tony Dungy.

Dunn, J. 2007. *Ray Lewis*. Broomall, PA: Mason Crest.

This book documents the experiences of a great football player named Ray Lewis.

Robinson, S. 2007. *Safe at Home*. New York: Scholastic.

This books describes the events of a little boy who uses baseball as a means of dealing with the recent loss of his dad.

Theme: Identity

Asim, J. 2006. *Whose Toes Are Those?* Nashville, LB Kids.

This board book teaches babies and toddlers about their body parts.

Hudson, C. 1990. *Bright Eyes, Brown Skin*. Orange, NJ: Just Us Books.

This book celebrates the beauty of African American children.

Lewis, E. 2003. *Creativity*. Boston: Sandpiper.

This book tells the story of an African American boy who appreciates the similarities and differences of a Puerto Rican friend named Hector.

Theme: Family

Keats, E. 1998. *Peter's Chair*. New York: Puffin.

This book tells the story of a little boy named Peter, who is upset about the changes that are happening in his family due to a new sibling.

Smalls, I. 1999. *Kevin and His Dad*. New York: Little, Brown Books for Young Readers.

This book shares heartwarming moments that a young boy named Kevin experiences with his dad.

Steptoe, J. 2001. *In Daddy's Arms I Am Tall: African Americans Celebrating Fathers*. New York: Lee and Low Books.

This book celebrates fathers of African American children.

Theme: Historical Fiction

Bunting, E. 1996. *The Blue and the Gray*. New York: Scholastic.

This book tells the story of two friends, one black and one white, who are living in the post–Civil War South.

Curtis, C. 2009. *Elijah of Buxton*. New York: Scholastic.

This book tells the story of a young boy named Elijah, who struggles to understand and overcome the atrocities of racial injustice while traveling on the Underground Railroad.

Curtis, G. 2001. *The Bat Boy and His Violin*. New York: Aladdin.

This book talks about a little boy named Reginald, who plays classical music for the worst team in the Negro National League. His music helps the losing team to win against the powerful Monarchs.

Theme: Fantasy

Myers, C. 2000. *Wings*. New York: Scholastic Press.
  This book tells the story of a young boy named Ikarus Jackson, who is ridiculed by many people in his neighborhood about his wings.
Pinkney, B. 2000. *The Adventures of Sparrowboy*. New York: Aladdin.
  This book shares the experiences of a superhero named Sparrowboy as he handles minor wrongs in his neighborhood.
West, T., and L. Uhley. 2007. *Double Trouble*. New York: Scholastic.
  This book tells the experiences of a streetwise kid who uses his superpowers to combat foes in the city.

Theme: Biography

Gottfried, T. 2001. *Earvin Magic Johnson: Champion and Crusader*. London: Watts.
  This book documents the life of legendary basketball player Earvin "Magic" Johnson.
Grimes, N. 2008. *Barack Obama: Son of Promise*. New York: Simon & Schuster Books for Young Readers.
Weinstein, M. 2013. *Play, Louis, Play! The True Story of a Boy and His Horn*. New York: Bloomsbury.
  This book showcases the childhood experiences of the great musician Louis Armstrong.

Theme: Animals

Bannett, K. 2008. *Not Norman: A Goldfish Story*. Somerville, MA: Candlewick Press.
  In this book, a little boy is initially disappointed when he receives a goldfish named Norman for his birthday. Later, he learns to appreciate the pet.
Davis, P. 2000. *Brian's Bird*. Walnut Creek, CA: Shen's Books.
  This book tells the experience of a boy who receives a parakeet for his eighth birthday. The bird escapes and eventually finds its way back to safety.
Lee, S., and T. Lee. 2005. *Please, Puppy, Please*. New York: Simon & Schuster Books for Young Readers.
  This book shares the experiences of two toddlers and their new puppy.

Theme: Music/Rhythm

Ehrhardt, K. 2006. *This Jazz Man*. New York: Harcourt Children's Books.
  This book uses jazz rhythms to teach the reader about various people and events associated with jazz.
Marley, B., and C. Marley. 2012. *Every Little Thing: Based on the Song Three Little Birds*. San Francisco: Chronicle Books.
  This book uses song to communicate a positive message to children.

Smith, C. 2002. *A Musical Journal with the Boys' Choir of Harlem*. New York: Jump at the Sun.

This collection of poems captures the feelings and expressions of music in various forms.

Theme: Community

Crews, D. 1998. *Bigmama's*. New York: Greenwillow Books.

This book tells the experiences of a young man who visits his grandmother's house in Florida.

Myers, W. 1997. *Harlem*. New York: Scholastic.

This book celebrates the wonderful sights, sounds, and people in Harlem.

Tarpley, N. 2009. *Bippity Bop Barbershop*. New York: Little, Brown Books for Young Readers.

This book describes a boy named Miles's first experience at the community barbershop.

~

Appendix B:
Sample Choice Board

Create a commercial about the text	Create a song and dance about the text	Write a summary of the events in the text
Create a poem about the text	Personal choice	Dramatize your favorite part of the book
Create a timeline of the major events in the text	Create a digital story to retell the major events in the events in the text	Create a mind map of the events in the text

~

Appendix C:
Sample Graphic Organizers

Brainstorming Web

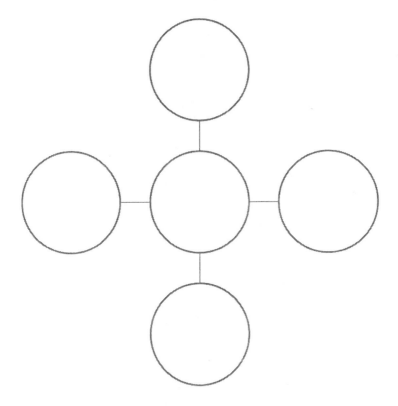

Venn Diagram

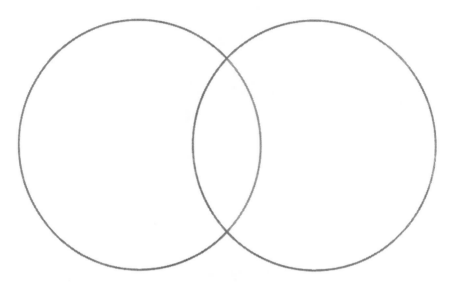

T-chart

Advantages	Disadvantages

Story Map

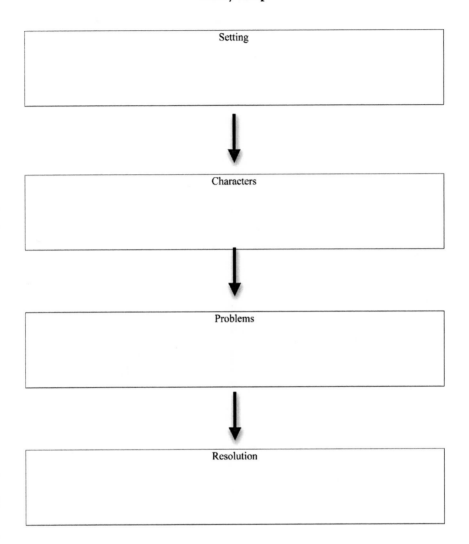

Prediction Map

Page Number	What do you think will happen?	What clues support your prediction?	What actually happened?

Sequence Diagram

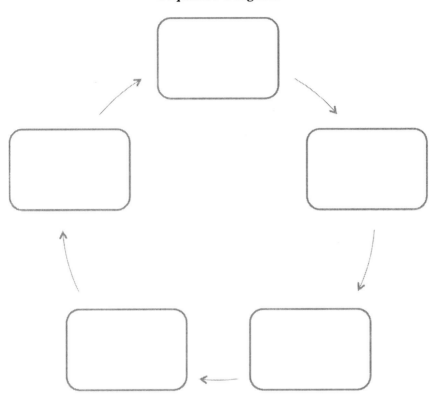

Text Connections Chart

Page Number	Words or Phrases	Text to Self Text to Text Text to World	Explanation

Vocabulary Map

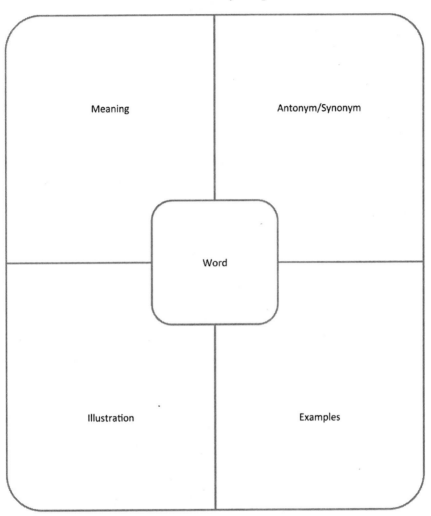

Drawing a Conclusion Diagram

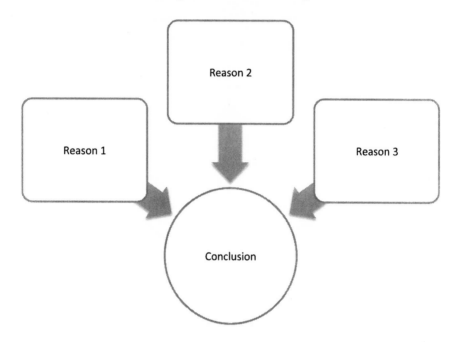

Main Idea and Supporting Details Diagram

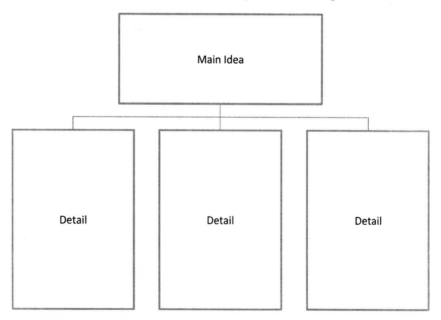

~

Appendix D:
Reading Interest Inventory

Name _____ Date _____

Part I: General Reading Preferences

Directions: Please answer each of the following questions in detail. Use the back if necessary.

- How do you feel about reading? Please be honest!

- What do you like about reading?

- What do you dislike about reading?

- What is your favorite book? Why?

- What kinds of texts to you like to read at home?

Part II: Genre Preferences

Directions: Circle the types of books you enjoy reading in your spare time in the left column. Provide an example in the right column for every genre you circled.

Genres	Examples
Biography	
Science	
History	
Poetry	
Supernatural	
How-to	
Folktales	
Travel	
Mystery	
Adventure	
Fantasy	
Realistic fiction	
Historical fiction	
Science fiction	
Humor	
Animal stories	
Other	

Part III: Activities Preferences

Directions: Check the box that best describes your feelings about each activity listed in the first column.

	I really enjoy this activity very much	I somewhat enjoy this activity	I do not enjoy this activity
Reading adventure stories			
Crafts			
Playing outside			
Playing with puzzles			
Playing board games			
Playing video games			
Reading about animals			
Watching television			
Reading chapter books			
Reading how-to books			
Writing stories			
Writing reports			
Reading about science			
Reading about funny things			
Reading about gross things			

	I really enjoy this activity very much	I somewhat enjoy this activity	I do not enjoy this activity
Reading about the weather			
Riding a bike			
Riding a skateboard			
Dancing			
Reading comic books			
Reading about friends and friendships			
Writing poetry			
Reading fantasy books			
Playing sports			
Reading about fashion			
Reading newspapers			
Playing an instrument			
Reading about famous people			
Reading about aliens and space			
Drawing and painting			
Listening to music			
Cooking food			

	I really enjoy this activity very much	*I somewhat enjoy this activity*	*I do not enjoy this activity*
Reading about sports			
Going to the movies			
Watching movies at home			
Reading about real places			
Reading about cars and motorcycles			
Using the Internet			
Going to the library			
Going to church			
Spending time with friends			
Going swimming			
Going to an amusement park			
Going to museums			
Reading fictional stories			
Reading nonfictional stories			
Talking on the telephone			

~

Bibliography

Baroody, Alison E., and Jennifer Dobbs-Oates. 2011. "Child and Parent Characteristics, Parental Expectations, and Child Behaviors Related to Preschool Children's Interest in Literacy." *Early Child Development and Care* 181, no. 3: 345–59.

Beard, Roger, and Andrew Burrell. 2010. "Writing Attainment in 9- to 11-year-olds: Some Differences between Girls and Boys in Two Genres." *Language and Education: An International Journal* 24, no. 6: 495–515.

Brozo, Bill. 2010. "Boys Will Read When Their Interest Is Piqued." *Reading Today* 27, no. 6: 7.

Clarke, Olivia. 2005. "Engaging the Digital Natives in Learning." *Primary and Middle Years Educator* 3, no. 3: 20–25.

Collins, Tandria. 2006. "Culturally Responsive Literacy Instruction." *Teaching Exceptional Children* 39, no. 2: 62–65.

Cooper, Carey E., and Robert Crosnoe. 2007. "The Engagement in Schooling of Economically Disadvantaged Parents and Children." *Youth and Society* 38, no. 3: 372–91.

Davila, Denise, and Lisa Patrick. 2010. "Asking the Experts: What Children Have to Say about Their Reading Preferences." *Language Arts* 87, no. 3: 199–210.

Fisher, Douglas, and Nancy Frey. 2012. "Motivating Boys to Read: Inquiry, Modeling, and Choice Matter." *Journal of Adolescent and Adult Literacy* 55, no. 7: 587–96.

Gaines, Lawrence. *A Teacher's Guide to Multisensory Learning: Improving Literacy by Engaging the Senses*. Alexandria, VA: ASCD, 2008.

Gambrell, Linda B. 2011. "Seven Rules of Engagement: What's Most Important to Know about Motivation to Read." *Reading Teacher* 65, no. 3: 172–78.

Ghiso, María Paula. 2011. "Writing That Matters: Collaborative Inquiry and Authoring Practices in a First-Grade Class." *Language Arts* 88, no. 5: 346–55.

Giles, Gail. 2008. "Wanted: Male Models." *School Library Journal* 54, no. 12: 48–49.

Graham, Steve, and Michael Hebert. 2011. "Writing to Read: A Meta-analysis of the Impact of Writing and Writing Instruction on Reading." *Harvard Educational Review* 81, no. 4: 710–44.

Hattie, John, and Helen Timperley. 2007. "The Power of Feedback." *Review of Educational Research* 77, no. 1: 81–112.

Husband, Terry. 2012. "Why Can't Jamal Read?" *Phi Delta Kappan* 93, no. 5: 23–27.

Jaleel, K. Abdul-Adil, and Alvin David Farmer. 2006. "Inner-City African American Parental Involvement in Elementary Schools: Getting beyond Urban Legends of Apathy." *School Psychology Quarterly* 21, no. 1: 1–12.

Karsbaek, Barbara. 2011. "Writer's Workshop: Does It Improve the Skills of Young Writers?" *Illinois Reading Council Journal* 39, no. 2: 3–11.

King, Kelley, and Michael Gurian. 2006. "Teaching to the Minds of Boys." *Educational Leadership* 64, no. 1: 56–61.

Lintner, Timothy. 2011. "Using 'Exceptional' Children's Literature to Promote Character Education in Elementary Social Studies Classrooms." *Social Studies* 102, no. 5: 200–203.

Lleras, Christy, and Claudia Rangel. 2009. "Ability Grouping Practices in Elementary School and African American/Hispanic Achievement." *American Journal of Education* 115, no. 2: 279–304.

Logan, Sarah, and Rhona Johnston. 2010. "Investigating Gender Differences in Reading." *Educational Review* 62, no. 2: 175–87.

McCartney, Sarah J. 2008. "The Impact of No Child Left Behind on Teachers' Writing Instruction." *Written Communication* 25, no. 4: 462–505.

McGarrell, Hedy, and Jeff Verbeem. 2007. "Motivating Revision of Drafts through Formative Feedback." *ELT Journal: English Language Teachers Journal* 61, no. 3: 228–36.

Merisuo-Storm, Tuula. 2006. "Girls and Boys Like to Read and Write Different Texts." *Scandinavian Journal of Educational Research* 50, no. 2: 111–25.

Miller, Donalyn. 2012. "Creating a Classroom Where Readers Flourish." *Reading Teacher* 66, no. 2: 88–92.

National Center for Educational Statistics. *National Assessment of Educational Progress.* Washington, DC: U.S. Department of Education, 2011.

Noguera, Pedro A. 2012. "Saving Black and Latino Boys." *Phi Delta Kappan* 93, no. 5: 8–12.

Painter, Diane D. 2009. "Providing Differentiated Learning Experiences through Multigenre Projects." *Intervention in School and Clinic* 44, no. 5: 288–93.

Parsons, Seth A., and Allison E. Ward. 2011. "The Case for Authentic Tasks in Content Literacy." *Reading Teacher* 64, no. 6: 462–65.

Protacio, Maria Selena. 2012. "Reading Motivation: A Focus on English Learners." *Reading Teacher* 66, no. 1: 69–77.

Rashid, Hakim M. 2009. "From Brilliant Baby to Child Placed at Risk: The Perilous Path of African American Boys in Early Childhood Education." *Journal of Negro Education* 78, no. 3: 347–58.

Regan, Kelley, and Sheri Berkeley. 2012. "Effective Reading and Writing Instruction: A Focus on Modeling." *Intervention in School and Clinic* 47, no. 5: 276–82.

Sang-Keun, Shin. 2008. "'Fire Your Proofreader!' Grammar Correction in the Writing Classroom." *ELT Journal: English Language Teachers Journal* 62, no. 4: 358–65.

Senn, Nicole. 2012. "Effective Approaches to Motivate and Engage Reluctant Boys in Literacy." *Reading Teacher* 66, no. 3: 211–20.

Stauffer, Suzanne M. 2007. "Developing Children's Interest in Reading." *Library Trends* 56, no. 2: 402–22.

Sugai, George, and Robert H. Horner. 2009. "Responsiveness-to-Intervention and School-wide Positive Behavior Supports: Integration of Multi-tiered System Approaches." *Exceptionality* 17, no. 4: 223–37.

Tatum, Alfred W. 2006. "Engaging African American Males in Reading." *Educational Leadership* 63, no. 5: 44–49.

Tyler, Kenneth M., and Christina M. Boelter. 2008. "Linking Black Middle School Students' Perceptions of Teachers' Expectations to Academic Engagement and Efficacy." *Negro Educational Review* 59, nos. 1/2: 27–44.

Webb-Johnson, Gwendolyn. 2002. "Are Schools Ready for Joshua? Dimensions of African-American Culture among Students Identified as Having Behavioral/Emotional Disorders." *International Journal of Qualitative Studies in Education* 15, no. 6: 653–71.

Williams, Terrinieka T., and Bernadette Sánchez. 2013. "Identifying and Decreasing Barriers to Parent Involvement for Inner-City Parents." *Youth and Society* 45, no. 1: 54–74.